MW01284955

ITALIAN COOKBOOK
Famous Italian Recipes That Satisfy

Baking, Pizza, Pasta, Lasagna, Chicken Parmesan, Meatballs
Desserts, Cannoli, Tiramisu, Gelato & More

Mario Mazzo

MARIO MAZZO RECIPES

11/2419

First published June 14, 2016

ISBN-13: 978-1985803381
ISBN-10: 1985803380

SOME RECIPE PHOTOS FROM THIS BOOK

See them in color on my website at mariomazzo.com/recipe-photos

Sicilian Pizza

Ricotta Cheesecake

Mazzo's Garlic Bread

Calzone

Tiramisu

Biscotti

See these and other color recipe photos at MarioMazzo.com

DISCLAIMER

Disclaimer of Warranty, Limit of Liability & Terms of Use

This book is for entertainment purposes only and is provided as is without warranty. The publisher and author do not take responsibility for any adverse effects or consequences such as but not limited to: allergies, choking, eating contaminated food, and getting either burned or cut for example. Please do not use, make or eat any food ingredient published in this book if you or others are allergic to it. Readers are strongly urged to take all precautions to ensure that all ingredients are fresh and fully cooked in order to avoid the dangers of food borne illnesses. A medical professional should be consulted before making any changes to diet or daily routine. The information and recipes in this book are not intended to provide dietary advice or recommendations whatsoever. Additionally, the recipe cooking times may vary and require adjustment, depending on the accuracy of the specific appliance you are cooking with. All efforts have been made to ensure that the information in this book is accurate and complete. The author and publisher do not warrant the accuracy of the information, text, and graphics contained within this book. The author and publisher shall not be held responsible for any errors, omissions, or contrary interpretation of the subject matter herein. Every word in this book is solely the opinion of the author. You are at your own risk. If you do not understand this disclaimer please have someone explain to you. Mario Mazzo is not a doctor or medical professional. He is only a chef and author. He does not offer medical or health advice. Every word in this book is strictly his opinion and is not to be interpreted as medical advice.

Please Read If Under 18 Years of Age

For minors (anyone under 18 years of age), do not attempt to follow any recipes, directions in this book, or eat any of the food ingredients listed in this book, unless you are under the direct care and supervision of a parent or legal guardian and they have taken full responsibility to prepare, cook, and serve food for you. Please have your parent or guardian with you at all times, and ask them to read this "Disclaimer" section before asking for their help or having them help you.

PAPERBACK & DIGITAL VERSIONS

Save a tree and buy an e-book and store them on compatible electronic devices!

This book contains over 30 popular recipes including a salad, garlic bread, fresh homemade pasta, extra sauce recipes, and sandwich recipes that were added throughout the year of 2017.

Digital book customers can refresh and update their previously purchased eBooks to latest edition whenever the author or publisher makes changes to the eBook edition.

SEE PHOTOS & PIC TUTORIALS

Some photos of recipes from this book with others can be seen in color at MarioMazzo.com/recipe-photos

Pictures are purposely placed on MarioMazzo.com and not in this book in order to keep the price of Digital and Paperback books affordable for all! All photos are large and of high quality.

Plus, on the blog page of my website MarioMazzo.com/blog you get:

Fun Sicilian Pizza Picture Tutorials

*Regular Sicilian Pizza

*Brazilian Sicilian Turkey Pizza

Take My Mini eBook as a FREE GIFT

Thanks for purchasing my book. To show my appreciation, I'd like to give you a free mini eBook.

<u>BOTH OF MY SECRET SAUCE RECIPES ARE IN THIS BOOK</u>

TOMATO SAUCE RECIPE & ASIAN BROWN SAUCE RECIPE

"I've never given these 2 recipes to anyone"

Get this Book at MarioMazzo.com/free-book

Special Offer for Amazon Paperback Owners of this Book!

If you buy this book in the paperback version, you can now also **add the digital Kindle eBook version** to your library for a super low **discounted price** with ***Amazon's Kindle Matchbook program***.

JOIN MAZZO'S RECIPE CLUB – IT'S FREE

WHAT YOU GET

- A Free Mini Book by Mario called "Secret Ingredients" - only available at mariomazzo.com
- Email alerts when important changes are made to recipes in the e-books you own by me. This way you can easily update your digital books to the newest version for free that have this feature, and you'll also get alerts when new cookbooks are published.
- You'll also get other things like an occasional recipe or cooking tip from time to time.

WHAT YOU WON'T GET

You definitely won't be bombarded with tons of emails trying to entice you to buy anything. Actually, I rarely send out emails. But when I do, it's usually something important or helpful like a kitchen tip or recipe or link to my blog page.

This email club is totally free so become a part of it now. Just head over to my website. You can join on my homepage and get your free book at the same time.

It's an email-based subscription, but your privacy is highly respected, so I will not give it to or sell it to anyone, for any reason.

CONTENTS

ABOUT THIS BOOK

Spending Money at Restaurants

Are you tired yet of spending much of your hard-earned cash at restaurants? Eating at the most affordable Italian restaurant chains can cost over $100 for a family of four. $25 or $30 per person isn't too much, but it's definitely not the $8.99 the commercials showed on TV. This book will help you make the same recipes for a fraction of the cost of eating out! Most quality cookbooks use the same traditional recipes that the Celebrity Chefs use in their cookbooks. Now you can save your money by purchasing this book since it has tried and tested famous recipes that received a high score ranking from those that used them!

Cost at Home

I'm estimating that the cost to make a large tray of lasagna or Chicken Parmesan from the recipes in this book should be under $25.00 and can feed 6 to 8 hungry people. This is about an 80% savings to eat at home.

The Recipes

The recipes in this book were carefully chosen, written by me personally, then tweaked for easy reading and cooking. They are "not" random copies taken from average websites, then pasted into a Wannabe cookbook. You can be confident to know that all of the recipes in this cookbook are "ranked highly" and have been rated at between 4 and 5 stars by the many who have cooked them. That's why I call them 5 star recipes. Since I sell my book at a very affordable price, that doesn't mean it's inferior. Not all cookbooks are created equal. They don't have to cost $15 to $30 with fancy color pictures. You just need the delicious recipes!

For Vegetarians, Vegans, & Carnivores

For those of you who love Italian food and are reading a sample of this book, but are a bit indecisive about buying it, listen up. I have good news for you. Well probably not so much for the vegans but hopefully for the vegetarians. Most of these recipes can be veggie friendly just by substituting out the meat with your favorite veggies. Most Italian recipes can be customized this way since the main ingredients are usually the tomatoes or cheese. So, for vegetarians that don't mind subbing out the meat for other ingredients then this book should be okay, but probably not so much for vegans since they will need good tasting milk and dairy substitutes and everyone knows those can be a challenge to find.

Meat & Dairy Eaters

When making a dish that requires meat or dairy, I always recommend using fresh organic grass-fed meat and dairy products. Not only does this taste better, but for it's good for health reasons. If I ever forget to mention the word "organic" you can always assume that you should try to buy all your beef, chicken, and dairy products under the organic label, when possible, even if they cost a few more dollars.

This Book is Great for

Beginners and even chefs with a little experience. Beginners can feel at ease completing these recipes due to the easy to follow directions with all of the tips, notes, and shopping advice provided. If you own the digital version of this book, the file size is very small so you can bring it with you when you travel, since it takes up hardly any space on your device. This is a great help for professional chefs that want easy, quick access to the ingredients, proportions and ratios.

A chef's blessing goes out to all of you cooks out there. Hope it turns out perfect!

THE AUTHOR

If you are wondering a little about who Mario Mazzo is, I'll give you the short version here. I've been cooking for a while, just over 40 years now. I still enjoy making traditional recipes but like to also come up with some of my own creations from time to time. I love cooking all sorts of stuff including: American, Italian, Thai, Chinese, Middle Eastern, and even a famous Brazilian Fish Stew called "Moqueca."

I've learned all about Moqueca Fresh Fish Stew while living in Brazil for a while. And I can tell you that it is delicious. I usually make it with Mahi-Mahi.

I started cooking as a very young teen as many kids do these days. But in the 70's when I was a teen it wasn't that popular. I started with the usual Tuna Melt Sandwiches, Scrambled Eggs, Spaghetti, but graduated into more advanced dishes a couple of years later like Lasagna and fresh Apple Pie from scratch.

No pre-made pie shells here. My home-economics High School teacher who knew how to make great food since she graduated from a famous culinary school. Now-a-days besides making Italian food, my other favorite foods to cook are: Chinese Stir Fry dishes, Gourmet Sandwiches, Omelets, Soups, French toast, Desserts, Potato Pancakes, and some other things. I've even learned to cook Thai food when visiting Thailand.

The most requested dishes I make are: Pizza, Calzone, Desserts, Stir-Fried Chicken with Brown Sauce, Fried Rice, Lo Mein, Eggplant Parmesan, Lasagna, Fettuccine Alfredo, Risotto, Penne alla Vodka, and also Grilled Sandwiches with the melted cheese of course.

I feel that creating great food doesn't happen by accident. Delicious food is the result of a combination of several things. There are many factors, but the top three in my opinion are:

(1) Having some decent taste buds.

(2) Knowing the basics about cooking and which ingredients complement each other.

(3) Using quality ingredients.

I usually lecture people about tasting their food as they cook it. If you don't taste your food while it's in the process of cooking then how in the world will you know if it's good enough to eat or serve to others? There are some exceptions obviously that you have to wait for until they're finished baking or cooking.

So, I like to taste, taste, taste, whenever I can. This is my best bit of advice to everyone, especially new chefs.

Having halfway decent taste buds or finding someone that does certainly helps.

Whether I use traditional recipes or develop new ones, I search for the freshest, highest quality ingredients. And if using a recipe, I try to search out the best traditional recipe for that dish. Later I can tweak it if I want.

After a few years, 40 in my case, you get to know my way around the kitchen a little, and can make adjustments according to taste.

But it's usually a bad idea for beginners to tamper with recipes that are good ones and close to perfect. I've learned this the hard way of course due to my experimental nature.

Usually less is better, unless you're making something more exotic like Thai or Indian cuisine, which calls for many various of herbs and spices.

Being born and raised in New York and New Jersey, I've learned about food and culture at a very young age.

I've worked in a few diner and family type restaurant kitchens as a cook when I was in my 20's. This means people actually had to pay to eat the food I cooked. But did they come back again? Hmmm, that's the question.

A few years later I took up bartending by going to the popular school in NJ. After getting my degree with the little signed wallet card they give you, I tried my hand at a few restaurants and country clubs.

I left the northeast though because I had enough of it back then, and had the pleasure to live in several cities throughout the U.S. and also international cities such as long stays in Mexico, Brazil, and Thailand with a few short stops in other countries like, London, Italy, France, Israel, Malaysia, Philippines, Singapore.

I've spent about 5 months living in Thailand. Thai food is one of the best in the world, and Thailand has some incredibly skilled chefs. They also have a ton of great Indian chefs there too, since that country is in close proximity to India. The Malaysian food I've had when in had in Penang, and Kuala Lumpur was super delicious and hard to find a bad meal.

I picked up some great Thai recipes and techniques by attending a cooking school in the great city of Chiang Mai which is well known for excellent Thai cuisine. These guys don't mess around. When it comes to making great food, they're the best and always use fresh ingredients.

The teachers from the school take you to the local outdoor fresh food market and show you how to shop for these hard to find items, so that you can make the ultimate fresh ground curry pastes that not many Thai restaurants in the USA even know how to make. They usually but the paste or powder pre-made.

Forget buying the dried curry powder which is such a crime really. The fresh curry paste is where it's at! The powders you buy at the store don't come close to the flavor of the real thing.

When living abroad I've gained many fans for my Organic Sugar Chocolate Chip Cookies. They're usually gobbled up in seconds, by those international cookie monsters.

I have lots of amusing stories from my travels that I'd like to write about one day in a book, but in this book, I scratched out one or two of them.

I like art, music, nature and spiritual things. I'm a chef, author, and now the creator of Mazzo's Recipe Club. It's a free recipe club keeping my readers and fans updated with new things, book revisions, cooking tips, and also offers an occasional recipe alert when I post a new recipe to my blog page. You can find articles I've written there on my blog or other pages.

My site is mariomazzo.com and it has some cool things for you to check out. There's even a kitchen tools / shopping ingredient page for finding some items you may not see at grocery stores like cannoli shells, for example.

On the kitchen tools page you'll find a link to a Cannoli website. There you can get everything Cannoli like supplies, molds, tools, shells, t-shirts and other things.

I'm planning to release many more cookbooks in the near future. You can follow me on Twitter & Facebook for news and updates. Read more about me if you like in my mini bio at the end of this book.

AUTHOR TRIVIA

Born
Brooklyn, NY, USA in the early 60's
Favorite Food to Eat
Italian, Chinese, Thai, Japanese, Middle Eastern, Mexican, Sandwiches, Fish, BBQ
Favorite Food to Cook
Italian, Chinese, Thai, Grilled Sandwiches, Omelets, Pancakes, Potato Pancakes, Desserts
Favorite Desserts
Anything Chocolate, Cannoli, Tiramisu, Cheesecake, Italian Rainbow Cookies, Cinnamon Rolls
More Favorite Desserts
Brooklyn Blackout Cake, Éclairs, Cinnamon Rolls, Pies, Donuts, Ice Cream, Toffee, Cookies
Favorite Music
Classic & Southern Rock, Folk, Jazz, Classical Music, Italian, Brazilian, 60's
Favorite Outdoor Things
Mountains, Beaches, Fresh Air, Animals in Nature

INTRO

Did you buy this book for the recipes only? Hey, no problem. The extra info is in the first half of the book.

Don't waste any time, just go to the recipe section near the middle.

But if you'd like some extra reading material, I've included lots of stuff for you to browse through, including stories and other kitchen info. I hope you enjoy!

This book has the popular Italian food and desserts that you'll find in many restaurants around the world. I know many of you haven't tried making these great classics yet at home, so don't you think it's about time?

I've included super easy directions to make them a breeze. Most of these dishes aren't difficult to make, so just put on your apron, and start cooking with me. Oh, wait you may need to look at the ingredient lists and get to the store first and then you can make your friends and family smile with these quality classics, and be cooking like a pro in no time.

The recipes in this book are 5 Star Quality and there's really no reason they shouldn't turn out great.

The high-quality ingredients suggested in this book are healthy so you can make better tasting food immediately.

See the chapter in this book "Italian Cooking 101" to learn more about which ingredients are essential to making delicious Italian food.

Something you won't find in this cookbook, are common ingredients such as: margarine, soy oil, canola oil and other things that may not be so great for your health. Manufacturers of these products have made claims that they're good for your health, but that's usually not the case. They care about one thing only and it's certainly not your health! You know, it's all just the two M's which are money and marketing. Also, you'll never see suggestions to use of a microwave oven in this book.

There are none in my kitchen. I use a toaster oven to heat small portions like a square of lasagna, a slice of pizza, crisp things up a bit, or for small batches of freshly baked cookies. In this book you'll find a variety of flavors, so whatever you're in the mood for is now basically at your fingertips. All recipes in this book are delicious and it's tough to beat them.

Most Celebrity Chefs usually use these same exact ingredients and the same basic proportions when making these classics, so save your money on those expensive cookbooks and let me teach you how to make them.

I may even teach you a few new tricks that you never heard of before, as some reviewers have stated.

All recipes in this book are great, so it's difficult to pick favorites here. The red sauce dishes are incredible as well as the non-red sauce recipes like: Fettuccine Alfredo, Mushroom Risotto, Chicken Piccata, Chicken Marsala, and Angel Hair Pasta with Pesto Sauce.

The pizza and desserts are fantastic too. So try them all. When you taste them, you'll know why I say these are the best of the best versions of these famous classics.

Once you've tried these classic recipes, you can substitute most of the meats and veggies to make your own custom creations. For example, maybe you'd like to try and make a healthier lasagna, sort of like half Eggplant Parm and half Lasagna, instead of using the traditional meat sauce.

After learning the recipes, you can have more fun with them later when you feel like experimenting some to customizing them.

I've done my best to preserve these great classics with their amazing flavors. I really believe this book will become your favorite Italian Cookbook.

These 5 Star Italian-American Classics are as traditional as you'll find. There are no junk recipes filling up pages of this book, just some extra reading material in the beginning.

If you own the eBook version don't forget to refresh it once in a while, to receive all of the positive changes I may add in the future. By the way, there is no cost for you to update an eBook to the newest version once you've paid for it. Please check with the online retailer you purchased this book from to make sure it's possible.

PIZZA STORIES & MORE

I have a surprise for you pizza lovers out there who can't get enough pizza. The next 20 plus mini chapters contain lots of pizza talk.

There's pizza eating, pizza planning, pizza trivia, and other pizza things, including where to eat it and also the 10 Most Delicious Pizza Cities in the World.

Also I wrote about what it was like growing up next door to lots of old school pizza men in the 1960's. You know… the guys who make the best pies in the world.

These guys were characters. Some were macho, with the cigarette hanging from their mouth, others more humble but most were funny. But these guys were "real" Italians with heavy accents not wannabes.

They made the best pizza, and because of them the favors of Italy now reside in NY which has become the great pizza hub for the entire USA. So I hope you'll browse through the first half of this book in addition to reading the recipes. Let's begin.

PIZZA TRIVIA

How about some pizza trivia? Ready, Set, Go.

Q: What was the Name of the First Pizzeria in the United States?
A: Lombardi's

Q: Where was it Located?
A: 32 Spring Street, New York, NY

Q: When Did It Open?
A: 1905 (and is still operating today at the time of writing this)

Q: Around 2011: What was the Avg. Price for a "Slice of Pizza" in the New York City Area?
A: The Normal Range was: $0.99 - $2.75, but as high as $5.00 at a famous Brooklyn shop

Q: In 1969: What was the Avg. Price for a "Slice" in Most Brooklyn or NYC Pizzerias?
A: The Normal Range was: $0.30 - $0.35

Q: What's the Italian Word for a Person who Makes Pizzas in a Pizzeria?
A: Pizzaiolo / man
A: Pizzaiola / woman singular
A: Pizzaiolos or Pizzaioli / men
A: Pizzaiolas / women

I just call them all "the pizza man". It's easier, plus you rarely find a woman making pizzas in a restaurant. But you might a few times in your life, especially if you watch online videos.

1960's: THE PIZZA DECADE

The Scenario

Hippies and flower children remain scattered throughout the city as this decade nears its end.

I remember the funny clothing, especially the tacky flower print dresses women wore, and the weird looking 60's furniture, which now happens to be in style again.

I've seen it restored and selling for big bucks in antique shops and other stores. You know the bright red, or lime green and other crazy colors the sofas and products were back then.

As I walked down the streets of Brooklyn as a kid I'd hear the newest top 40 Motown songs fill the air, along with other new songs. Songs like The Doors, "Hello I Love You".

Speaking of music, a couple years later Led Zeppelin's Immigrant Song rang out its weird and kind of scary song intro, like a jungle call to all rockers.

It was like an alarm clock going off every hour on the hour, on all New York AM Top 40 Radio Stations.

Besides classical music in the 60's, the most popular genres of music playing on the radio back then were only a few like: Motown, Classic Rock, The British Invasion, Folk, Singers and Standards, and an occasional Instrumental song mixed in. Did I miss one?

No, there wasn't Hip-Hop or Alternative Rock yet. Things were simple then.

The enticing smell of freshly baked bread, cheese, tomato sauce, and oregano scented the air in front of each pizzeria.

It gave you a peaceful feeling that everything was okay. And how could it not be?

All you had to do was take a walk down the street and this fragrant smell was your personal tour guide leading you to the pizza ovens.

You had instant access, to all of the New York Pizza you could eat.

The smell on the street was from what we call Pizza, and it was gaining popularity as the most addictive, comfort food ever.

Its craze quickly took hold of a 90 mile radius and New York City was its center. It quickly found its way into restaurants throughout the whole country.

EYE of THE PIZZA STORM

The 90 mile radius I speak of is what I call "the eye of the pizza storm". I've coined this phrase because after the first pizza shop opened in NY in 1905 the pizza hurricane started spinning, which was only a few miles away from where I was born.

Many of the Italian owned pizzerias perfected these pies, thanks to the Italian immigrants making them. They started popping up in all 5 boroughs of New York and into New Jersey, Long Island and the rest of the area.

The NY pizzas probably tasted better than the last generation of pies made by these same guys from Italy a few years earlier.

As their skills improved so did their pies! One good thing about a chef is that their food usually improves through time, as their recipes and skills are perfected.

From Long Island, NY to Philadelphia, PA you're bound to find some great tomato and cheese pies every square mile.

They are fresh, hot and ready to eat. Unless you're out in the sticks somewhere, as us NY'ers or Jersey Boys say. Even though I was a youngster by the end of the sixties, I clearly remember the details, like it was yesterday. Things were very different then. No decade is perfect but things kind of felt that way back then.

After all I was only a kid without responsibilities yet. Life was simple even though there were protests and political things taking place in a big way.

The memories of what it was like to eat a fresh hot slice of pizza inside those little pizzerias, or pizza parlors as we called them, is what I'll focus on in the next couple of chapters.

PIZZA with CULTURE

The pizza was so good back then that words like delicious doesn't really cut it. Eating pizza in Brooklyn or NYC back in the 60's and even the 70's was a special experience. It was more of a special experience.

If you've had slices of a pie from New York City or its 4 surrounding boroughs, most will agree that it's difficult to beat, except for the pizza in Italy of course. It's a close call.

When I've had the rare pleasure of watching someone eat NY Pizza for the first time, it's a priceless experience to watch their face and eyes light up after the first bite. Now, I'm not talking about NY style pizza only. I'm speaking of watching them eat actual NY pizza inside a New York pizzeria, just so that were on the same page.

Have you ever heard the song "Saturday in the Park" by the band Chicago? Listen to the part of the song about the man selling ice cream singing Italian songs. This song also reminds me about the NY Pizza eating experience back in those days. In case you don't know the song, it's about popular Central Park located in the center of New York City (not Italy).

The song was written in the 1970's. And I happen to know exactly what these guys were singing about in that song. I've had my own personal experiences hearing these Italian merchants sing. They had great voices and could really belt out a tune when the mood hit them. Some of them reminded me of opera singers.

Not only did they sing outside around the park while selling ice cream, and Italian ices but they'd sing indoors too when the mood hit them, while standing in front of the hot pizza ovens.

Sometimes you'd hear them burst into 30 second episodes of opera like singing which was a treat. I'm guessing these were parts of their traditional songs. It was a well-rounded eating experience that you can't forget. .

I'd bet that listening to a live accordion player on the streets of Italy with a fashionably dressed monkey on his shoulder wouldn't compare to this pizza eating experience. Plus monkeys like to steal food.

NEW YORK PIZZA vs. TEXAS PIZZA

While living in Texas for a while, I've heard Texan parents say to their kids, "Hey, Y'all-Wanna-Pizza-Fa-Dinner-Taaa-Night?" And the kids get so excited chanting, "Yeah, Pizza-Pizza!"

And of course you know that we're talking about pizza from a fast food chain restaurant, right? In 1994 for the first time I tried the all you can eat pizza buffet for $2.99 from a popular Texas chain restaurant.

It was interesting to say the least. You get all you can eat pizza, pasta and salad for under 3 dollars back then. Now it's probably $4.99. The pizza wasn't so great, but you really couldn't complain too much because it was for under 3 dollars.

I laugh thinking, if these kids only knew what real pizza tasted like, they'd never want to touch the fake stuff again. Adults and children can figure out the difference between good and bad pizza, when given the opportunity. The only problem is that they haven't had the real thing yet, because most would have to spend about 30 hours driving on a long road trip to get a taste of the good stuff. All Texas food is not bad.

I managed to find a couple of decent Chinese restaurants in north Texas. And there are literally thousands of great Mexican restaurants in the Lone Star State.

Here's a puzzle. Texas is to Mexican as New York is to _____. But when it comes to pizza in Texas, you're probably not going to find an acceptable slice there. But wait a minute, I've had an okay slice one time in north Texas. I can't recall the name or the town or the pizza shop, but it was probably located somewhere near Lewisville, Texas. And the owner was so proud of his average pizza. And believe me, to get an edible slice in Texas is a difficult task.

I remember some details of about the transaction. When I was at the counter trying to pay, the owner wouldn't let me because he gave all of his first time diners their first couple of slices free. I told him that his pizza was the best I've had in Texas. He told me he knew this and that's why he doesn't mind people their first meal on the house because he knows they'll be back. Texans have manners don't they? I'll say so. It's not just because they don't make you pay for food, but they're great people most of the time. Just watch out for them on the road.

They are totally different when they get behind the wheel of a car. They go from Dr. Jeckell to the other guy real fast. Those same sweet people become crazy drivers and lose all their southern hospitality. Y'all Texans that live in a big city like Dallas know what I mean right? Get out of their way and don't sit at that traffic light after it turns green too long or they will blast their horn at you.

Back to pizza now. Sorry Texas but you didn't make the top 10 pizza list. But you guys do have something to be proud of and you know what that is don't you? You guessed it. It's the Mexican food. But when I'm dipping my chips into the salsa bowl please don't let me see you scratching the inside of your ears with your car keys. It's not very appetizing. I love Texas but I'm not joking about the car keys.

I actually witnessed this a couple of times. Don't worry, I've seen worse things from a NJ Italian pizza man while standing on a ladder in front of the counter, while getting some pizza boxes. I won't get into any details though since this is a family book but would be a good story to add to another book of true stories if I ever write one.

About the great Tex-Mex food in Texas, the quantity and "quality" of the Mexican restaurants there is impossible to beat. In my opinion and many others, they rank #1 for Mexican food in the US. I know this isn't a Mexican cookbook but I just wanted to share this with you hungry people new to the Dallas area looking for good places to eat. If you want a special treat, look for a Mexican restaurant that features a live Mariachi band that plays certain days and hours of the week. These places usually have decent food. My favorite place is downtown Dallas.

They're loud though, so make sure you're not sitting too close to the band, or you'll be shouting at each other. For Texans or visitors to Dallas, since I can't recommend any good pizzerias there, I can at least try to hook you up with some good Mexican restaurants. So, if you want to know some of my favorite for Mexican spots the Dallas Metroplex shoot me over a message to my Twitter or Facebook.

HOW GREAT is PIZZA?

Growing up in Brooklyn in the 60's was great, and even though I was on the young side I clearly remember it like yesterday. I've got lots of stories about people, places and things, but I'll try to stay on the subject here which is pizza and food.

I've eaten so much great food in NY, NJ and even PA by the time I was eighteen, but what really stood out was eating pizza during the late 1960's as a kid. I still remember the taste and the difference.

The pizza flavor of the 60's and 70's was something unique. It was somewhere in between a true Neapolitan and a NY Pizza. Now a days you will be getting a NY Pizza when in New York.

This is a good thing, I'm not complaining one bit but the version of pizza they served in the late 60's was incredible. It was thin, very wet, almost soupy, and the flavor couldn't really be explained.

And remember, I've tasted pizza when visiting Napoli, Italy and also Palermo so I know a little about pizza, blah-blah-blah.

In Brooklyn, around 1968-1969, a slice of pizza at the local pizzerias cost about $0.30. It truly was the best tasting pizza on the planet and hasn't improved since then, regardless of what others may tell you.

I don't even think the pizza I've had when in Italy was better than the 60's and 70's pizza from Brooklyn and also NYC. Please don't get me wrong, the pizza in Italy was delicious and it would be a close call.

The bottom line was that in 1969 you got a slice of pizza for 30 cents that's flavor was unmatched. It didn't get any better unless you factored in the coke. Yes the drink, not the drug. The fountain draft coke was so tasty in the 60's and 70's, and everyone who remembers it will tell you the same.

It had a different sweeter, purer syrup. The soft drinks today don't come close. Then its main competitor who came along even had a super great taste and its syrup was richer too back then.

Now the cola served in the old skinny light green glass bottles was incredible too. We preferred the fountain drinks though when eating at the pizzeria because my Dad swore that it tasted better.

Who really knows though, maybe it was psychological. I think he was correct though, because most of the machines seemed to pump more of the main ingredient (which is the syrup) than you'd get in a bottle. It was all good though.

Between that ice cold drink in the tall slim paper waxed cup and the hot slice of pizza, FauGedaBoud. Eating this hot dripping juicy pizza and drinking that cold drink was always the best event of the day or even the whole week.

There aren't words to explain it to those who are not enlightened by this experience. The only way you'd understand is if you had similar experiences.

If you could travel back in time to the 60's, or download the flavors into your mouth via internet you'd agree 100% of the time.

No, I'm not exaggerating for the sake of this book. Every good New York and Jersey boy or girl will tell you how things were back then. Of course I'm speaking about the ones who truly love pizza of course. The rest don't have a clue, but I wish they did.

So here's the good news now. Although you can't get the same exact original flavors today when walking around NYC, Queens, Bronx, Staten Island or Brooklyn, you can however get something very close to it.

There are many pizza shops that will still blow your mind, and many creative entrepreneurs have started pizza tours of their favorite pizzerias in the city.

So although some may argue with me about the old vs. the new, which is totally fine, I am always open to tasting new pizza and seeing how it ranks compared to the old time pizza from about 50 years ago. I've had some delicious pizza that comes very close to quality stuff I've had in my childhood and teen years though. So my expectations are always high and I try to stay positive!

EATING BROOKLYN PIZZA in the 1960s

I remember in the late 1960's eating pizza with my Dad. Sometimes I was in the car with him in between his errand runs and he'd like to stop by a pizzeria for a snack.

He'd drive up to the front door of a small pizzeria then ask me to go in and buy pizza slices for both of us while he parked the car.

Out of his wallet would slide 2 one dollar bills. Yes that's right, you young kids out there. Two dollars fed both of us lots of food. These days you can't even get a drink for $2 in most places.

After handing me the 2 bucks, he said something like this. "Get me 2 slices and a medium coke with this dollar, and whatever you want with the other dollar." I'd get the same thing trading these valuable 2 dollars for 4 slices of pizza and drinks for our lunch. There was even a little change left over.

INSIDE the PIZZA PARLOR

After walking into the pizza parlor, the first thing I recall was the smell inside. It was incredible. Next, I'd see the pizza man standing at the counter watching me walk up to greet him.

With a broken accent he'd ask me, "Whaa-Chu-a-Want?" I'd reply with something like, "4 regular slices and 2 cokes." You always would say regular so that the guy knew that I wasn't asking for Sicilian.

The man would hit those register keys and they'd ring out loud at the end showing the final price, which was around $1.80 or something close to it. It was a very fair price, right? It's all relative I guess.

Immediately after the man took the money, gave my change back and put the slices into the oven, I'd see my Dad walking through the front door.

He'd come over and ask politely if I ordered everything. "Yes, and here comes our pizza now out of the oven now", I'd reply. Dad would then help carry the hot pizza on thin paper plates while I carried the ice cold drinks to the table.

Lots of small shop owners had music playing on AM radios which sat under the counter next to the old fashioned cash register.

You'd hear Diana Ross or British Invasion music, and all other 60's stuff, unless they preferred singing the Italian songs from their homeland. In that case it was silent in the shop until you'd hear their next live inspired song.

PIZZA COSTS BACK THEN

Most stores were small back then because there weren't really any large corporations or franchises yet. Rent in Brooklyn was cheap, about $75 per month for a nice 2 bedroom apartment at that time.

30¢ for a slice of pizza and 20¢ for a cup of coke wasn't such a great deal if you think about it.

It may sound like a bargain to you but it wasn't really compared to the pay rate then. If you divide the rent of an apartment by about 500 it should give you an idea of what a slice of pizza should cost now as compared to back then.

For example if you take the average rent of an apartment New York being 1500 per month and divide it by 500 you get $3.00 per slice.

Now calculate the average rent back in the 60's of around $100 and divide that by 500 and you get .20 cents.

DON'T BURN YOUR MOUTH

After my Dad and I would sit down to eat this very hot pizza, we would have to wait at least 30 seconds before even trying to shove these hot slices into our mouths.

Much patience was required and lots of fanning and blowing took place because these slices were blistering hot. It wasn't the same pizza you eat today.

This pizza was very wet with lots of cheese and sauce, without much dough so it trapped the heat and you'd get a nice blister in your mouth if you didn't wait.

It was frustrating but worth it to wait as long as you possibly could because the smell of the pizza was so tempting.

I'd watch my dad take his 2 slices and stack them on top of each other making his double-decker. About 10 years later in the movie Saturday Night Fever, I noticed that John Travolta did the same thing in the opening scene of the movie as he walked down the street eating his two slices.

My dad of course did the New York fold with that double-decker since he was also born in Brooklyn. NY pizza is very thin so I guess it works with two pieces.

He'd then proceed to eat his slices but this seemed a bit extreme to me. He's known for doing crazy things and if you gave him a weird stare he'd also give you one back.

He'd then continue to devour this two story pizza sandwich which only took him a minute or two. This guy really knew how to eat. I won't dare tell you how he ate his ice cream at home.

I ate my pizza slower obviously since I was only a kid, and while he sipped on his coke washing down the pizza, I finally finish mine. He'd then politely ask, "You done?" And we'd head back to the car.

It's funny how I can't remember the drive back home or much else that happened after those fun pizza eating adventures. My brain remembers the good things and not the boring stuff in life so much.

ALMOST 50 YEARS LATER

After thinking about this now, which is almost half a century later, it seems more like a dream than reality. It's funny how selective our memories are. Remembering the amazing pizza want hard to do I guess. And the serious impression it made was understandable.

When I say that the flavor of this pizza was incredible, I mean it. The place my dad took me to was a great one. But the 90% of the dozens of pizzerias scattered around the boroughs served delicious pizza.

If you want to find a decent one these days, all you have to do is look at the online reviews for pizza and you find lots of good ones. A little trick you can do is look up different pizza tour companies and see which shops are on their list if they disclose that info.

Or better yet, take a pizza tour with these guys, and let them be your personal tour guide. They know where the good pizza is. The 20 and 30 year old pizza guys that served me the pizza back then are mostly now all in their 70's and 80's or no longer around.

Some of the shops probably still remain and hopefully the founders have passed on their secrets to the next generation.

Most of the pizza in those days tasted very similar in the surrounding neighborhoods. They kept the recipes simple and uniform, not trying to be too unique, and it paid off in a big way.

You couldn't complain about any of it. Some had more oregano than the next, or some had a little more dough, but it all was amazing. Even the worst pizza in Brooklyn back then was delicious. When you've had the best pizza or any food for that matter your taste buds seem to remember it. Don't they? At least mine do.

FOR RESTAURATEURS w/o PIZZA

Are you a restaurant owner that doesn't serve pizza yet? I highly suggest you learn how to make pizza pies. Many people love ordering a pie for lunch or dinner.

If that doesn't interest you then it's no biggie I guess because there are plenty of places these days people can go for a slice or a pie.

But if you want your share of the pizza pie, then you must learn how to make one. Making pizza may seem intimidating at first, but it isn't that difficult to make.

Just start off with a regular stand mixer and if all goes well for you, you can upgrade later to a larger commercial mixer later down the road.

Getting the dough just right may take a couple of tries, but when you master the two most important elements, perfecting the dough and choosing the proper temperature to bake at, the whole town will be eating out of your hand, literally.

Well, that is of course if you use good tomatoes and cheese on top of that homemade dough.

So to all you restaurateurs, and everyone else reading this, it's not that difficult to make a half way decent pizza. Forget about the awards for now, just try to make an average or above average pizza.

But whatever you do, don't make excuses purchasing the cheaper, inferior ingredients. Everyone can taste the difference. If you've got the ovens and counter space then go for it. After a few mistakes you'll be a pro.

Keep reading, to see which are my favorite top 10 pizza cities, I've enjoyed eating pizza in. This may encourage you to see that there are cities all over the world that make good pizza and anyone can do it.

Remember these top picks are from my first hand experiences from eating pizza from around the world.

It's not from some cheesy pizza blog that was hijacked!

I not only make the stuff, I like to find others that make it also, and eat it whenever possible. I've actually lost weight eating pizza a couple of times per week so that's why I call it a healthy food. Just make sure to eat lots of fruit and veggies during the week too.

So if you should ever decide to travel to any of these cities you can do a quick search online and try to locate the best pizza shops via the many reviews posted online by pizza lovers.

See what you can learn and try to produce a tasty pizza on your own. When it's good enough for you then it may be good enough for others to eat too.

TOP 10 PIZZA CITIES in the WORLD

I've had the pleasure of tasting lots of pizza from around the world. Maybe you'll find my exploration interesting and maybe not, but if you love pizza the way I do, then I'd pay attention to this chapter.

Out of the thousands of different pizza slices and pies I've sampled so far, here's my personal pizza cities favorite list. I'm sure there are many other cities out there that are known for great pizza but I've either never been to them or did not think they were as good as these cities below.

I feel that I'm qualified to speak on this subject because to date I've traveled to around 28 of the United States, and also to 12 other countries not including stop-over cities in airports.

I've decided to put NJ and PA on the same line because they're like brother and sister and so close to NY. Although some feel that that NJ or PA deserve their own spots on the list, there are so many great pizzerias in both states and they can be considered equal in quality.

But I probably prefer NJ pizza because I know where many of the great shops are there since that is where I lived for many years. And just over the bridge from NYC you've got so many great pizza shops.

Just know that although a calzone is really considered a pizza that's folded over without sauce inside, some of the best calzones I've had were in New Jersey. And one of my favorite places to eat a piping hot calzone for years was located in a small pizzeria located in the hills of NJ.

1ST Place is A Tie between New York & Italy

1 New York, NY USA – So much amazing pizza incl. the other 4 boroughs of NY + other cities.

1 Italy (Napoli + Palermo) I've had really great pizza in both of these great cities.

2 New Jersey + Pennsylvania, USA – Have eaten so much great pizza from both of the two.

3 Israel (Jerusalem + Tel Aviv) Israel is for Real. I found so many great pizzerias there.

4 San Francisco, CA, USA – I've had delicious pizza there, and wanted to try so many more places.

5 Chicago, IL, USA – I've had Chicago style pizza in 2 pizzerias, and it was cheesy delicious!

6 Los Angeles, CA, USA – I've had decent pizza at 2 locations there.

7 Fort Lauderdale, FL, USA – I've found 1 place with delicious pizza but there used to be another.

8 Phuket, THAILAND – I've had good pizza at an Italian owned restaurant there.

9 Brazil (Copacabana Beach, Rio de Janeiro) - Brazil made this list by the skin of its teeth.

Stats for the Top 10 Pizza Locations

There are 10 locations but NY and Italy share the same number 1 spot.

These cities were chosen to represent their country or state. The top 10 picks were based on a few contributing factors such as: flavor, texture, and similarities to the pizza served in Italy or New York.

Keep reading to learn more about why these locations made the list.

This list was created for your amusement and just in case you decide to visit any of these places you can be encouraged to take the time to grab a slice of pizza there. If you're not tire of pizza chat yet then keep reading.

Why These Top 10 Cities Made the List

New York: I love you're pizza, like millions of others that eat it all the time, you'll know why NY tops the list. It's known for what I love to eat the most, which is its NY style pizza. So when you're in New York City you have to try a fresh hot slice or two or three if you've never tried any yet.

There are plenty of places to enjoy good pizza in all 5 boroughs of NY. You can also get a decent Italian meal in restaurants in Little Italy, NYC which is near Greenwich Village. Greenwich Village has a few great pizza shops, but if you're adventurous you may feel like hitting some places in Brooklyn or other the other boroughs.

My favorites are pizza from NYC and Brooklyn. You can easily jump a train from NYC to Brooklyn and be there in less than an hour. Brooklyn also has some great other ethnic food you should try like Russian or Polish food. There's a large Russian community there with delicious bakeries that are delicious!

Italy: Is the mother of Italian food. It's hard to find a bad place to eat there. Not only can Italians cook well but they know how to bake a pizza which is a very important skill to have.

Palermo Sicily was a nice city to visit and I've enjoyed great pizza there. But they are not only known for Sicilian pizza but so many fantastic desserts there like Gelato, Cannoli and other little snacks.

The pizza I've had in Napoli aka Naples to us Americans was my favorite though. Napoli is known for their pizza as Palermo for their Sicilian Pizza and so many great desserts. **See pictures on my website from Italy!**

Whether it's a pizza in Napoli, Sicilian Pizza from Sicily, or the myriads of mini pastries sitting behind glass cases inside the cafés of Palermo, just about everything you could every ask for, is at your fingertips in Italy. They have the best food, super sports cars, and classy clothing. Plus many more things. Sei magnifico!

New Jersey & PA: The food in New Jersey and Pennsylvania is incredible. I always say yes to both, and especially in New Jersey, unless you want a Philly Cheese Steak of course or head down to the Amish Country in Lancaster County for the best delicious fried chicken you've ever had.

The Pizza in New Jersey is little thicker than NY Pizza but the flavors are very close to the NYC Pizza if you know where to go for a slice. From shops in Hoboken, to the countless pizza shops scattered down all of the Jersey boardwalks from Asbury Park to Atlantic City you're bound to get an amazing slice.

The pizza in Philadelphia is great too but I prefer New Jersey Pizza over both. But when in Philly don't forget to eat a Cheesesteak sandwich! I haven't spent that much time in Philly but their food is great too. Philly is only about 90 minutes from NYC. So it makes a great weekend trip when in the NYC area.

Israel: This was the biggest surprise to me. I found so much delicious pizza in Jerusalem at a few pizzerias. I even managed to find some great pizza in Tel Aviv at one place near a shopping mall.

How can pizza be so good all the way over there? I don't really have the answer but if I had to guess, I'd say that for starters, it's only about 5 hours by plan from Italy. And second, many Israeli's or people that Immigrated there come from New York and know how to make great pizza.

Besides eating pizza in Italy, New York, or New Jersey I would say that the pizza in Jerusalem comes in next on the list for flavor and quality to the real thing. Now Jerusalem is the copycat pizza of New York.

I've had great pizza at least 3 places in Jerusalem maybe 4. Whether you opt in for a kosher slice of pizza, or want to try a non-kosher slice, the Holy Land may be the answer to your prayers when far away from home.

So it just goes to show you that Israeli's are not only good at inventions, but can also copy things that seem just like the original like New York Pizza and Fish & Chips from a small shop found inside the shuk market in Jerusalem!

San Francisco: Is on the map and is a well-known city for great food. I wish I had more time to try out more food there but even with the very limited amount of time I was able to locate a delicious pizzeria.

I've heard there are many more but unfortunately I only had time to check out one place. So far San Fran is 1/1. Who knows, if I had more time there they could have stolen the # 3 position?

Chicago: Yes the people of the windy city will get a place in the top 5 of the list. Of course the natives from Chicago will say that they deserve the # 1 spot on the list, but everyone from the Tri-State area laugh at this.

Do they have great pizza, of course they do. But does it rank right below Italy? Come on now, let's be realistic here okay? Their pizza, which is very unique and so delicious so Chicagoans can be proud they make this list!

They know how to make some really great pizza and it definitely has its own unique characteristics. When you're in Chicago get a Chicago deep dish style pizza and also a stuffed one! I get hungry just thinking about it now.

Chicagoans can make a deep dish pie like nobody else. You can't go wrong in that city with either a regular or stuffed pizza. Just ask any Chicagoan where the good stuff is, and they'll probably be more than happy to point you in the right direction. I've enjoyed pizza in 2 pizzerias while there a few years ago and was very happy with it.

Los Angeles: Actually it has a few good pizza shops but Dorothy, you'll know that you're not in NYC anymore. I say head to San Francisco when wanting a better slice of pizza. I'm not disrespecting you LA and you did make this list but the pizza was not what I hoped for, but I did get a couple of good slices!

Just make sure you check some online reviews before wasting your time driving to a pizza shop so you're not disappointed. You may find a decent place or two like I did. The pizza however was tasty enough at both spots to rank where it did on the list but I wouldn't write home about it.

Florida: They rank in the top 10 because of Fort Lauderdale alone. The whole state of Florida ranked in the # 3 spot a few years ago, due to an amazing pizza shop on the Daytona Beach Boardwalk but it's not there any longer, and Florida took a big drop in rankings because of this.

This Daytona Pizza was next best to NYC pizza but it's not there now on the corner of the boardwalk, has relocated and after trying a slice of pizza at the new location was not satisfied with it.

The good news is that there is a pizzeria in Fort Lauderdale that pulls the weight of the whole state of Florida. But this is a hard job to do. I've heard it stays opened 24 hours per day which is great when you want a fix

Across the street you have the beach and that's why I names a chapter in this book FLORIDA OR BUST.

I don't usually refer people to specific pizzerias but because things can change fast. The shop can change ownership or just not produce good pizza anymore. But since this one has been consistent over the years, is opened 24 hours/day, and is right across the street from the beach,

I always recommend to anyone in South Florida. I'm not connected to them in anyway, and do not get paid for referrals. I just like their pizza. See their details in the Florida or Bust Chapter.

Phuket, Thailand: Phuket is a state of Southern Thailand that features many beach towns. Patong beach has many great places to eat since it's one of the most popular resort towns in Thailand.

It made the cut because of a small Italian owned restaurant I visited a couple of times that's located about a 5 minute walk from Patong Beach in Phuket, Thailand. You can sit down and enjoy a decent pizza or an Italian meal from an Italian owner.

I didn't eat too much pizza in Thailand even though I was there 5 months because who really wants pizza when there's so much great Thai food everywhere. Well I do, but I wanted to try all of the Thai Food at as many places that I could and got hooked on it!

When real Italians make a pizza it's kind of hard for them to screw it up. But anything is possible I guess. Everything at this restaurant was pretty good. His pizza was good enough to make this list, and when you're that far away from Italy or New York and want a halfway decent pizza you really complain.

Copacabana Beach, Rio de Janeiro: It's so famous that a nightclub in New York was named after this beach town in Rio.

Later Barry Manilow sang about this club in NYC, and this song must have made him a ton of cash due to its catchy name melody. I've actually walked inside a hotel that reminded me of that song.

The hotel I'm speaking of is the Copacabana Palace Hotel in Copacabana Beach, Rio.

It's really difficult to find a good pizza in Brazil, but I stumbled into a gem one afternoon in Copacabana. About a 5 minute walk from the beach sits a little pizzeria that's a few blocks from the Roxy Cinema.

I never expected this pizza to make this list. The pizza was so good that I purchased 2 slices. It came in last place however. Rio made it to the top 10 list due to its New York flavor.

I call this the miracle pizza because it's the only pizza in all of Brazil I've had that reminded me of NY Pizza. Sorry, Brazil, I wish I could give you a better rating but I can't.

Being # 10 on this list should make you proud because it's not easy to get on this list. So take what you can get. But don't get too comfortable because as soon as I can find a replacement for you, you're history.

Update: In 2017 I visited my favorite spot in Rio and in June of 2017 the pizza did not look very edible the day of my visit.

I tasted a small piece and I was correct. Maybe the pizza had a bad day. It was old and stale looking like it was sitting 5 hours or more.

I think the owner needs a good manager watching over his fancy store. But it just goes to show you how quickly things can change in the food world. So their time on this list will probably be ending soon.

Brazil now has a contract with The Food Network channel obviously since it airs now in their country on cable TV in the homes of millions of Brazilians. Maybe there's hope for Brazil after all. I wish they will get their act together soon and make authentic pizzas.

Brazil all you really have to do is, Use hotter ovens, learn how to make authentic pizza dough, use real good tomato sauce, and better Mozzarella cheese and I'm sure you can pull this off. Just don't be lazy anymore. There is no laziness in pizza.

Most pizza shops I don't remember the names to but if I wanted I could look at online maps and get them. One day I may publish them for all to see, but until them I only give out the name to a gem that stands out in Florida for now listed in the Florida or Bust chapter.

PIZZA TASTING AROUND the WORLD

I've had pizza in so many cities and even on an Italian cruise ship which was super delicious. Here is where I ramble on a bit about the pizza I've had in some of these cities and countries.

Eating Chicago Pizza

Now when it comes to Chicago Pizza, Chicagoans will of course say that I'm biased since I grew up in New York, but that's just how those guys are over there.

They'll claim to have the best pizza in the US, blah-blah-blah, but most of us that have eaten pizza in New York City at a good pizzeria will of course disagree.

I feel that they were ranked properly. Actually they are the only city I've included that did not qualify as regular pizza. It's actually not right for Chicago to be in this list in the first place. They should be ranked # 1 on a separate list all together for deep dish pizza. But I put them on this list because their pizza is really good.

When it comes to crafting a true Chicago deep dish or stuffed pizza you guys do it right and can't be beat. You've earned my respect and have your spot on this list. When arriving in Chicago for the first time, of course I had to try out their pizza. I was pleasantly surprised with the taste at both Giordano's and the other pizza joint I sampled pizza at. Both pizzas were delicious and loaded with tons of cheese, especially the stuffed pizza.

The cheese inside the stuffed pie oozed out like a volcano when you tried lifting up a piece, which is a very good thing. I do have to say, that after growing up in Brooklyn, it may be a challenge for me to live in Chicago though, and for the obvious food related reasons.

Why? I might enjoy the change for a while eating a different style of pizza, but I'd probably get bored with it after a few weeks and crave the real stuff. But who knows anything is possible.

When I visited Chicago, I would have probably enjoyed trying some of the other popular food the city is known for, but I was only there for only a couple of days, and didn't have time to go on any other food adventures besides the two pizzerias I ate at.

If there are any Chicagoans are reading this now, smile because you guys have some great pizza, but don't try to compete with New York or Italy. These are two totally different types of pizza and you shouldn't try to compare yourself with them.

You're flavors are more simple and bread is a lot thicker with a different flavor and texture. All great pizza connoisseurs know that Chicago pizza tastes great but is in a category of its own.

Eating New York Pizza

New York tends to dominate the pizza world at least in the U.S. In New York you've got a choice between thick, airy puffy Sicilian crust which is out of this world, and the traditional NY regular thin crust Pizza which is kind of similar to Neapolitan Pizza.

If you ever get a little bored with one you could easily switch to the other. Both have totally different flavors and textures. And because of this I could never get bored eating Pizza in NY or NJ.

The New York thin crust is based on the Neapolitan style pizza. It's a favorite with many and I never get enough of it, no matter how much I eat. It's thin enough to eat between 2 to 5 slices depending on how hungry you are.

I can usually put away 3, 4 or even 5 slices with no problem if it's my main meal. As a snack between meals one or two slices hit the spot. I can even eat this pizza for breakfast or a late night snack.

As a teen, living in New Jersey I've devoured piping hot extra-large 18 inch pies just about by myself. One night I remember eating 7 slices and saving one for later. New York and New Jersey are also known for their-Sicilian square pies. I like to walk into a pizza shop and order both, usually one slice of Sicilian, and one regular.

We call the thin pizza regular, or regular cheese FYI if you're not from that area. Pizza from Italy, New York, and New Jersey are my favorites. The differences between NY and Italy pies are this. The pies from Italy are baked for a very short time in a super-hot oven, usually wood burning, they have lots of sauce, a nice thin dough, with a few large pieces of cheese scattered. It tastes fresh and pure.

New York pizzas on the other hand have also a thin crust, but a lot more cheese which is evenly distributed, and it's usually shredded and baked a couple of minutes longer.

The Italian pies come in a small or medium size and not sold by the slice since they are on the small side. When I was in Italy the cost per pie was around 4 Euros which is an excellent price. NY Pizza is usually best paid for by the slice. The pies used are called slice pies, and they slice them into 8 large slices. These slice pies are super large and usually range from 20 inches to 22 inches.

Watch out Adam R., I can hold my own and a slice pie shouldn't be that much of a task for me if I'm hungry even though I'm getting older. Back in my teen years I could put one down very quickly, now it may take about 15 minutes or more.

So if you're even in the mood for pizza, and up for a pizza challenge you know where to find me. I know you're probably don't abuse your body too much lately with those contests and it needs a good long rest.

Eating Pizza in Brazil

After spending lots of time in Brazil I must say that Brazilians love their pizza. I say "their" because it's not normal pizza. I mean there's no sauce on it.

What's up with that? After speaking briefly with an employee at the counter of a Brazilian pizza joint, I walked out smiling and thinking that at least some Brazilians take pride in making real pizza.

Usually Brazil pizza doesn't come close to the pizza most are used to. It's basically bread and cheese. When a Brazilian asks me if I want pizza when I'm in their country, I rely with, "Do you mean bread with melted cheese?"

I'll give you the good, the bad and the ugly on Brazilian pizza here. Its important people learn about the differences when eating the Latin down under pizza. So here are the facts. Most Brazilians like doing things their own way and don't care about how others do things, even if their way sucks. Can you say improvement?

I'm talking about improving their pizza. The good news is that one can settle for a Rodizio of Pizza which I'll get into later. But if you find a decent pizza in Brazil which is few and far between, you are definitely going to pay for it. When I say pay, I mean pay. Pizzerias in Sao Paulo or Rio de Janeiro charge about R$50 to R$70 for their close to authentic pizzas. This comes to between: $18 - $35 USD for a pie depending on the exchange rate at that time. And these pies are only medium in size. I mean you can eat the whole thing by yourself.

This is evident when it comes to their pizza. If you like baked bread with cheese or white pizzas then you will love Brazilian Pizza, but if you are addicted to tomatoes like me then you probably won't.

Brazilian pizzerias use hardly any sauce. You can't really see it if you lift up the cheese and it's practically invisible. Only the places that try to make the real stuff use more sauce. To me this technically isn't a pizza.

There are a few places though in Brazil that try to make a real pizza and take pride in the universal pizza system of bread, sauce, and cheese.

One of the first times I ordered pizza in Brazil it was interesting. I freaked out kind of and can't forget it. It was one night at around 9:00 pm in a beach town across the street from the beach. When the pizza arrived, I asked the people with me, "Where's the sauce?" I thought they brought someone else's order. So I kept repeating, "Where's the sauce?" Do you know the old Wendy's commercial with the old lady asking, "Where's the beef?" Well this was me now asking, "Where's the sauce?"

I told the waiter that pizza is supposed to have tomato sauce on top, isn't it? And I was irritated because I was very hungry and had a craving for the real thing that night and did not know that Brazil usually makes a low quality pizza, using soft bread, cheap Mozzarella cheese and no sauce. I was ignorant about how they make pizza in Brazil since I didn't have experience there. Everyone acted like everything was fine, but it definitely wasn't. The waiter actually asked me if I wanted Ketchup. I laughed as you can imagine.

The best pizza I've had in in Brazil was back in 2012 in Rio de Janeiro. Unfortunately this real good pizza cost as much as 2 steak dinners. And it's not worth it so you just buy one or two slices instead of a whole pie, or you settle for going to a Rodizio instead where you can get all you can eat pizza for about half the price of what this guy charges for a whole pie.

What the heck is a Rodizio? A Rodizio feeds you like an all you can eat pizza buffet, but they bring it to your table instead. Every couple of minutes they bring a different type of pizza all for about R$35 which equals about $10 USD in 2017. They usually have pasta with dessert pizzas included too. And they're not bad if you don't need to have tomato sauce on your pizza.

Types of Pizza at Pizza Rodizios

Here are just a few varieties of pizza served at all you can eat Rodizios:

Mozzarella – A plain cheese pie.

Atum – is a basic Mozzarella pie with chunk dark Tuna sprinkled on top.

4 Cheese – This usually consists of Mozzarella, Parmesan, Catipury, and Gorgonzola or Provolone.

7 Cheese with French Fries and Steak - Usually has creamy fake Cheddar cheese as one of the cheeses.

Frango & Catipury - This one has Chicken and a type of Brazilian Cream Cheese.

Peru - Deli sliced Turkey breast on it. By the way, Peru is the name for Turkey down there.

Portuguese – This has Eggs, Sausage, Onions, Olives, and possibly another ingredient or two.

Margarita – Traditional basic pie with Basil but no tomato sauce but has a few tomato slices.

Mushroom Pizza – It has Mushrooms which they call champion.

Carne Seca – This has dried shredded steak on top.

You get the idea, plus there's even more including dessert pizzas like one that's called Romeo and Juliet believe it or not which is loaded with guava and mozzarella. If you go to one of these places you will walk out stuffed. So pace yourself. One place I go to puts Kit Kat bar pieces sprinkled on top of their chocolate pizza as a topping. These Rodizios usually cost between $9 to $13 USD these days per person.

More about Pizza Rodizios

They're fun and many Brazilians like to celebrate their birthdays at one. Most even give you 1 free meal if you can gather together 10 other friends on your special day. But that's a lot of people isn't it?

Pizza Rodizio Restaurants serve pizza and pasta, but there are regular Rodizios that specialize in meat and no pizza. At those you will get all types of beef steak cuts and chicken. The term Rodizio by the way means Rotation. That's because they keep bringing at rotation of a variety of things to your table.

I prefer the Rodizios which serve pizza and pasta since I don't eat red meat these days. But, if you eat red meat they're worth it because it's all you can eat steak and they are usually pretty decent and I've tasted a piece or two of steak from them.

At the Pizza Rodizios the waiters sometimes will bring French Fries to your table you can count on all types of pasta at most of them including pasta with shrimp. In Brazil you they usually do not clean the shrimp and it is the smallest type. I don't recommend eating this though because it stinks up the whole dining room when it leaves the kitchen. The shrimp are most likely not fresh and probably have tons of bacteria. So why not play it safe and pass when the waiter asks you if you if you'd like some. Hate to see you get ill on vacation.

You can also feel free to tell the waiter which pizzas are your favorites and they will tell the pizza makers. And that takes about 10 minutes to get to your table.

Some of these Pizza Rodizios can get noisy especially if they've got a couple of birthdays happening the same night. Dessert pizzas include: chocolate pizza, banana and cinnamon, crumb pizzas, chocolate calzone (which is nothing like it sounds). Chocolate confetti, and many others. Just remember the pies that we call white pizza in the US is what you'll be served in Brazil usually. So if you're cool with that then you'll be happy.

Rio de Janeiro Pizza Trivia

Did you know that in the state of Rio de Janeiro sometimes people eat their pizza with ketchup on it? Yes, of course this is totally gross, but when there is no tomato sauce in this stuff, so what's one to do? Ketchup is a quick fix for the people in Rio and they have to try to improve the flavor somehow, right? They also offer mustard. You'll see individual packets sitting in the table at most pizza restaurants. I usually use hot sauce at these places though.

Brazil Pizza vs. Thailand Pizza

If you are in the mood for a great vacation and want some halfway decent pizza after a long day in the hot Thai sun, then Phuket, Thailand may be the place for you. There's an Italian owned restaurant in the Patong Beach area of Phuket, and its walking distance from the beach. The pizza there was tasty enough to be called pizza and not too far of a walk from the beach.

The pizza in Chiang Mai, back in 2013 was also good. So Thailand beats Brazil's pizza in general. After all, you can live like a king in Thailand, as it's a cheap vacation spot, with great food and beaches. The only expensive part is getting there if you're from the US. Sometimes there are special air promos though.

Getting to Brazil by plane is expensive too most months of the year. So when deciding to go on a vacation, do your homework to see which country would be more suitable for you.

So if you're interested in tasting pizza in Thailand and Brazil it could be a close match but I thing that Thailand will probably win most of the time. I've had some okay Tiramisu in Brazil but I'm still waiting to see a Cannoli there. There are things I love about Brazil, but unfortunately food isn't one of them.

The food in Thailand is much better in my opinion. Besides amazing Thai food they've got authentic Indian food, some good fish and chips, American food, some Italian food, and others.

So as you'll see in my top 10 list that Thailand beat Brazil for pizza. I don't think I've had bad food once in Thailand and I have spent 5 months there.

The only place you can get a variety of international foods that taste good is in Sao Paulo, Brazil. It's like the New York City of Brazil.

The only type of food that will be difficult to duplicate outside of Brazil is a nice big cup or bowl of Acai. In a hot day it is the thing to go for and not an ice cream cone or Italian Ices.

Misc. Pizza Stuff

Pizza from Italy or New York has a certain flavor and when you're familiar with it, it's easy to it as measuring stick against other pizza in the world.

The combo of quality ingredients like flour, tomatoes and cheese along with knowing how to craft a pizza is what makes a great tasting pizza. All you need is a pizza checklist to make a great one.

If you don't even know what should be on the checklist, then you obviously are not going to produce an authentic tasting product.

Once you've eaten the real stuff from Italy or New York, you can always spot the counterfeits rather easily.

Don't try feeding me pizza made with GMO grown tomatoes from the USA with some cheap flavorless Mozzarella cheese and think I'm going to enjoy it. Sorry Charlie.

Just ask most celebrity chefs. They know about good ingredients and most of the time that's how most of them got to where they are now.

A good word spreads quickly through town when you have the real deal, and lines or a waiting lists are usually the norm all day long.

I'M PROUD to be a PIZZA SNOB

Yes, I'm a pizza snob. I hate to admit it but that's what I am. It's not my fault that I was born in Brooklyn and spoiled with the best pizza in the world. I'm learning how to be gracious to those making bad pizzas. It's not their fault that they never learned the process or where to buy the good ingredients.

This pizza I was raised on was carefully prepared and baked by Italian immigrants during the 1960's decade. These were the people that introduced me to pizza. Maybe on TV or in movies you've seen scenes where addicts sitting in a circle at the addiction group meeting state their name and a brief sentence before stating details.

Well for me, it would be great if I could find a group called Pizza Addicts Anonymous. And my intro would go something like this. "Hello my name is Mario, and I'm a pizza addict." Then they would all reply in unison, "Hello Mario, welcome." Then I would go on to telling them my story and say, "It all started when I was about two years old…"

When I 'm not in the Tri-State area I can tend to get a bit grouchy. I don't usually want to touch the stuff they call pizza in most cities, but I have to settle because there aren't many other options except I make it myself.

That's just the way life is sometimes. This is why I like to usually search for good pizza in whatever town I'm living in at the time and read online reviews to help guide me to the best places and save me time.

I can usually tell if pizza is good just by looking at it believe it or not. The pizza on the cover of this book gives the telltale signs of what a good traditional NY pizza looks like. First, you see the while cheese with medium brown spots showing you that the cheese is cooked to perfection. Then you have the visible red sauce spread all over, almost until the edge of the pie.

You'll also usually see a large air bubble or two on the edge of the crust. These are only the beginning tips. But to know if a pizza is really special you'll have to taste it of course. Usually the delicious smell inside a pizzeria will give you a hint if it's going to be good when you bite into it.

Pizza sitting under the glass display case like this doesn't usually last long in a high quality place because there are many customers all the time.

Although I have been fooled a couple of times because some of these pizza makers know how to bake a pizza properly but use inferior ingredients. That's why it's always best to order only one slice before ordering a second. If you don't think it's fantastic then you can go down the street to another and finish eating there.

Unfortunately, there are lots of Wannabe pizza shops that use inferior ingredients. Some of them even let this so called fresh pizza sit on the counter for hours, before selling its slices to their unsuspecting hungry guests.

They should at least eat the old pizza themselves or give it to the employees to eat and make fresh new ones for their paying customers.

You can find a halfway decent pizza joint outside Italy, NY or the Tri State Area but it may take some time. Sometimes a long time depending on which town or city you're in. And it's a lot more work, that's for sure.

I've had delicious pizza in 3 other countries, so I know it's possible to find a good one far away from home. You just have to sample lots of pizza from various restaurants and small pizzerias just to find the good stuff.

WATCH OUT for BAD PIZZA

No, you're not in the clear yet even if you live in New York. And you guys that live in NY probably know exactly what I'm talking about. Yes the bad pizza in NY most likely tastes better than the bad pizza from most of the other cities in the world or the good pizza actually, but, that still doesn't make it good.

I know this is surprising especially in a pizza hot spot such as NY, but there are many counterfeit places out there and sometimes you run into. Just remember there are counterfeits with everything in life. And pizza is no different. It may look like the real thing but it's fake. What I mean by fake is like using inferior ingredients. And the dough is not up to par. Just like fake reviews. When you see them enough you can usually spot them.

So be careful when looking to eat good food, especially pizza! When it sits too long it usually gets a yellow hard plastic like appearance. This simply means that the pizza shop isn't selling hardly any pizza there and there is a very good reason so avoid it.

There are even some places in NYC selling slices for only 99 cents and those places aren't so great. I've tried one of them just out of curiosity in 2011 when walking around NYC and it wasn't that great. But it wasn't terrible either. Just average, and usually better than pizza from other cities in the US.

Places that are super busy with a line of customers are usually a safer bet. You need to do your own research if visiting a city and want to find the best pies, even in NY unfortunately. The more good shops in a city then the more bad ones too.

There's a guy that I recently saw on TV that gives pizza tours. He takes you to about 3 or 4 pizzerias in the area so you can buy a slice at each. I then saw him in a documentary on one of the streaming channels. I think his name is Scott, but I'm not sure. This guy is a pizza freak, and knows his stuff.

Taking a pizza tour with a pro is probably a pretty cool thing to do if you have a limited amount of time when visiting New York and don't want to spend your time reading reviews.

It's a nice way to get to the top 5 shops around town As for me, I'd rather just look online for 5 minutes and write down the names of the top 10 places in town, then visit them when I'm out and about in those sections of town when it fits into my schedule for the day.

So have fun on the tour if that's what you decide to do. But don't sweat it. If you're in any of the New York boroughs which are: New York City (aka Manhattan or NYC), Brooklyn, Queens, Bronx, Staten Island you're bound to find a good slice of pizza probably just a few feet away from where you're standing.

HOW MANY PIES?

I'm used to seeing fresh pies coming out of the oven every 5 to 7 minutes in the better pizzerias. Lots of places have usually at least 4 to 6 pies in the ovens at all times. Well the good shops do at least because they sell so much pizza. Usually hundreds of pies per day.

If they're selling about 4 pies every 7 minutes you can imagine how many pies that is per day. Yeah that's a lot of pizza. These guys earn their living for sure and work hard. And it's not as easy as it looks, especially in the summertime, standing next to a hot oven all day. Sometimes during a slow period though between 2:00 pm to 4:00 pm, you may see the remaining slices of a pizza sitting under a glass case for 10 or 15 minutes which still isn't bad at all.

I actually like to eat also pizza that sits for 5-10 minutes. Why you ask? For you pizza newbies, it has a chance to cool off, and then has to be put back in the oven for 30 seconds to heat up again. This gives the bottom a perfect crispiness and crunch. So if you want the perfect slice, this could be the way to go. Either way, fresh out, or sitting for a few minutes, it's all good!

BACK in the 50's

You old timers out there probably remember much more than I do since I was only a kid in the 60's. And in the 50's pizza prices were so much lower right? I've heard that the slices in the 50's were in the 0.10 to 0.15 range and man, who wouldn't love to get a couple of fresh slices of pizza for a quarter? It's all relevant I guess because the rent in Brooklyn in the 60's was very low at around $75 to $100 per month for an apartment. I find it amusing to look online sometimes and see what the historical prices were for each decade going back about 100 years.

PIZZA is a HEALTHY FOOD

I sincerely believe that pizza is a healthy food, except for the gluten right? Call me crazy, but I never feel bad after eating pizza. I usually can stay fit and trim when eating pizza two times per week. But I know that it's not that good to eat bread and refined carbs that much so I don't go overboard lately.

Think about what the main ingredients consist of. You've got the flour, water, yeast, tomatoes, and cheese with a touch of olive oil here and there.

And that's about it really except of the salt, yeast and other little things. And no, if you're thinking that the fast food chain restaurant pizza is just as healthy, it's most likely not. They probably add artificial ingredients and dough conditioners to make the dough very soft after it's baked.

My belief is that I pizza is healthy because it isn't fried in oil like French Fries that sit in extremely hot oil which can cause a myriad of health problems. It's baked in an oven. Baked items are usually always healthier than deep fried. Fresh pizza made daily usually doesn't have dough conditioners if they make the dough by hand fresh, since it's not a pre-made pizza crust that you buy in the store.

The only thing that I can think of that would be healthier is if you could find a gluten free pizza shop. There's not that many of them, but they're out there. So try a slice one day at one of these places if they sell it by the slice. If not try a small pie to see if you like it.

Gluten is known to can cause health issues in many people, so you may want to lay off the real stuff and try some gluten free pizza one of these days. I tasted it fresh once and it was delicious.

I hardly could tell the difference in the flour. This isn't the norm and just wanted to share that with you, since I really enjoyed it.

MORE PIZZA TALK

New York Pizza

My favorite thing is to eat a hot slice of pizza straight out of the oven from a New York or New Jersey Pizzeria. Eating pizza as a kid through my late twenties was simply mind blowing because of where I ate it. It was inside the NY/NJ area. If any of you know what I'm talking about, I'm sure you'd agree.

Wow, that pizza tomato juice liquid sitting in between those hot layers of cheese and dough, you'll remember for a long time. If done correctly you'll get that juicy goodness along with the orange colored oil on top of the cheese that drips off when you fold the slice in half.

The orange oil is really only the fat from the cheese mixed with the tomatoes. Don't freak out. I used to think that this fat was so bad for you. I'd see people trying to absorbing it all with napkins before eating the pizza, and I started copying them like a parrot.

Later in life I found out that many natural doctors are now promoting good fats from things like: cheese, avocados, nuts, seeds, fish, butter and other foods. So I don't have to worry like I used to about eating all that cheese. Now I just have to remember to take my liquid magnesium drink to balance out all of the calcium I take in from cheese. You need both minerals you know.

I've heard that our body runs more efficiently when using fats for energy as opposed to carbs. So getting my energy and some protein from cheese seems to be working well for me instead of getting it from meat. Not many edible treats on this planet compare to pizza. The Italian pizza guys making these pies really know what they're doing.

Back in the day, as I recall, they spoke very little English and understood just enough to sell you pizza without any problems. If you're not bored yet, then keep on reading for more pizza talk. If you've heard enough about pizza for a while then nobody is keeping you from jumping to the recipes. I'll understand.

Too Many to Choose From

There must have been hundreds of Italian restaurants to choose from within a 15 mile radius of the center of NYC in the 70's. And there's probably a whole lot more these days. You'll always find a new gem by accident in NY, NJ and even PA, which are pizza hot spots and have other great food too.

Smoking, Cooking, or Both?

When the person in the kitchen making your food is from Italy and so are their relatives, you're usually in good hands. I can't remember when an immigrant from Italy made me bad food.

When growing around these immigrant pizza makers I would notice them doing things they shouldn't be doing while cooking, like smoking over your food, with a cigarette hanging out of their mouth. And other unsanitary things that I won't mention in this book. But their food was excellent. Dominick, Sal, Tony and the other guys knew how to make good food, even if they could have been a little more sanitary in the process.

Back in the 60's and 70's there weren't too many laws as today. You could smoke wherever and whenever you wanted, but probably not in the kitchen while making people's food. You didn't have to wear a seat belt when driving until the 80"s. Since things were a lot looser back then employees took advantage on occasion.

You can find some funny old cigarette commercials online and you'll see what I mean. Smoking was portrayed as a popular and fashionable thing to do, before the public was alerted to its hazardous effects. So the next time you think of the pizza guy smoking in the kitchen, here's an old cigarette commercial I found online for your entertainment at youtube.com/watch?v=NAExoSozc2c

FLORIDA or BUST

A little side note: I love eating in Epcot when visiting central Florida because there are lots of imported chefs from around the world making delicious food. They work in the related country restaurants scattered all around Epcot. If wanting some great international food without leaving the U.S. think Epcot if you live in central Florida. And if you're a FL resident and live close to Disney World you may want to get a season pass so you can go to eat at Epcot whenever you wish.

If you are ever in South Florida, grabbing a fresh hot slice of pizza at one of my favorite Florida pizza picks may be in order. The place is located in Fort Lauderdale, and is only about 100 feet from the beach. Just find Sunrise Blvd and take it all the way to the beach. This place stays open 24 hours per day, 7 day / week now according to their website. They're always consistent in flavor. The drive from the FLL airport is only 25 minutes, so if you ever have a long layover connection at FLL and have a craving for some good pizza, you may want to check out this place.

I've had pizza there at least a dozen times and every time it was consistently delicious. The slices are huge and cost about $2.50 each in 2012. They usually try not to raise the price too often which is good for everyone. I'm telling you about this place because it's difficult to find good pizza in Florida even though there are many New York pizza style restaurants down there.

Here's info taken directly from their website around December 3, 2017.I hear that they have great sandwiches too but I've only had their pizza. They have other locations in the USA. Their sandwiches are supposed to be great and they are famous for them as stated in TV.

Primanti Brothers

ADDRESS - 901 North Atlantic Blvd. (On the Beach) Fort Lauderdale, FL 33304

PHONE - (954) 565-0605

HOURS - 24 Hours - 7 Days a Week

TAKE a FOOD TOUR VACATION

I'd recommend taking a 3 week food tour vacation, focusing at least two weeks in the NY, NJ and Philly areas. Going when it's warm or summertime is best because you can do many things like going to the Jersey Boardwalk and eat some great pizza there. There are lots of other fun things to do within a few hours away, like taking a day to visit the Amish country for some amazing family style fried chicken with all the fixings'.

Maybe even head down south into West Virginia if you have some time but you probably won't. There's so much to do in the Tri-State area, especially in the summertime. You've got the great beaches and boardwalks in both New York and New Jersey along with Broadway shows in NYC, plus a nice Zoo in Philly, and all kinds of museums that you probably saw in movies, which is great for kids and also adults.

If on the west coast and only want to stay there then you can take a food tour from Chula Vista, CA which has great Mexican food all the way up to Newport Beach for an amazing Eggplant Parm Sandwich. And if you dare to go as high as San Francisco then you can get a much greater variety of world class food and pizza.

The amazing Eggplant Parm sandwich I mentioned was from a tiny little pizzeria in Newport Beach, CA. No it was not the one from a famous celebrity chef in town, but I'm sure that's a good one too.

PHILLY or BUST

When Philly Do as the Philadelphians Do - Get a Big Fat Juicy Cheese Steak Sandwich!

I know this section has nothing to do with pizza but I had to throw in for you sandwich lovers some extra info! I couldn't resist telling you, where to get a good cheese steak sandwich if you happen to make it down to Philadelphia one day. There's nothing like Philly when wanting a Cheese Steak Sandwich.

According to the internet the distance from Greenwich Village, in NYC to South St Philly is only 1 h 46 min, and **97 miles** by car via the NJ Turnpike and I-95.

Philadelphia just about fits inside the eye of that pizza storm being less than 100 miles away from NYC. So carnivores, whatever you do, spend at least a whole day and night in Philly if possible, and try some of those traditional Philly Cheese Steak Sandwiches.

Sorry vegetarians, but I'm with you most of the time as I try to eat lots of veggies lately but if I'm in Philly I'll break my non-red meat diet and eat a cheesesteak sandwich.

So when in the City of Brotherly Cheese Steak Love this is my treat. I mean, how can you turn down one of these great sandwich wonders? Last time I visited Philly, I've had 3 different Cheese Steak Sandwiches from 3 different shops. Below are the 3 restaurants I've sampled the cheesesteaks from. All were great!

(a) The famous Gino's Restaurant

(b) The famous Pat's Restaurant (right down the street from Gino's)

(c) An unknown little sandwich shop that sold groceries.

There's lots of non-famous sandwich shops all around the city that make killer Cheese Steak Subs. The little unknown place we tried was discovered thanks to online recommendations and reviews. It passed the test. It was just as delicious as Pat's and Gino's but all were a little different in flavor and the bread used.

Make sure to carefully plan a list of places to eat at in advance so you can be blown away. I wasn't too prepared but was able to pull off some good food when there. The more prepared you are the more it pays off to find good food.

It would be a sad thing to choose a dud restaurant when so many good ones are available, especially because you didn't charge your cell phone battery and couldn't surf the internet to get reviews and addresses. Maybe one day if I create a sandwich cookbook I'll be sure to squeeze in an original Philly Steak Sandwich recipe. Watching the chefs carve the meat and then chop it up on the griddle with onions and mushrooms before adding the cheese is always a fun thing experience. These sandwiches are lots of fun to eat but are messy. I hope you've enjoyed the first part of this book. Now let's get down to some serious business.

KITCHEN SAFETY

Safety in the kitchen is the most important thing when cooking and even when you're not cooking. It's extremely important, and hope you'll make it a priority too. Children can also benefit by learning these things at a young age when they cook with you.

A SAFETY CHECKLIST

WASH YOUR HANDS: Before and after touching all uncooked and even cooked or foods, especially eggs, dairy products, meat, fruit and vegetables. They may contain bacteria and viruses.

HEAT: Please be advised that some of the recipes in this cookbook require cooking at higher temperatures. Please be careful, even with low heat.

FABRICS: Never leave kitchen towels, oven mitts, or any item that can melt of catch on fire near a stove top or inside the oven, whether the stove or burners are turned on or not.

SHARP OBJECTS: Keep items like knives, blades grinders, blenders, processors, or anything similar out of the reach of children. Always keep them covered with a protective cover and unplugged.

PROTECT HANDS: Always use oven mitts or special kitchen gloves when handling any warm or hot pots, pans, dishes or anything else in the kitchen that has been heated.

WET OR THIN TOWELS: Never use a wet, damp or thin towel to handle a hot dish or pot. Water can be a conductor and easily burn your hands in a second or two through a thick wet or even a thin dry towel.

PROTECT ARMS: Not only protect your hands but watch your arms when sticking them into an oven. You can easily burn your arms on the sides of the oven. So wear a long shirt.

BOILING WATER: Be careful around it, especially when dropping things into a pot.

HOT LIQUIDS: Be careful around hot water, oil, or liquids, they can splatter or spill.

STEAM: Be careful when removing lids from pots and pans, especially pressure cookers. The steam alone can burn you, even if the liquid doesn't touch you.

BROKEN THINGS: Discard any broken or chipped plates, dishes, glasses, cups or anything that can cut you. The pieces can even get into your food or drinks. If the object is sentimental then try to glue it back together but retire it to a shelf somewhere in the house of kitchen, and don't use it again.

NON-STICK ITEMS: Using non-stick pots, pans and baking trays may not be suitable or safe at higher temperatures.

In our kitchen we've decided to get rid of all non-stick pots and pans. When reading the warning labels printed by the manufacturers in the past, they've clearly stated to only use them with low or medium heat.

Because of this reason alone we've decided it was easier to just avoid using them altogether, and eliminate the possibility of chemicals getting into our lungs or food. The non-stick coating, through stirring and regular use, can peel off and get into your food, so be aware

COMMON KITCHEN ACCIDENTS that HAPPEN

Getting cut by sharp objects, burned by hot dishes, pots, pans and liquid. Choking on food because of allergies or not chewing the food properly.

Food poisoning from dangerous bacteria like Salmonella or E-Coli. Botulism or Hepatitis from contaminated canned food or other prepared or raw food. Parasites from undercooked meats, especially pork can be transferred to you.

Please learn more about food safety. Safety is a very basic an important element when cooking so educate yourself. If you feel that you may need emergency care, do not hesitate to contact your local first aid or police department. For residents of the United States you can simply dial 911 for emergencies.

The author and publisher of this book are not responsible for accidents or situations that may occur. Please see the disclaimer page of this book.

TYPES of POTS and PANS

STAINLESS STEEL

I prefer using a stainless steel frying pan or pot whenever I cook. Not only should the food taste better as opposed to using the regular non-stick coated pans which so many use unfortunately, but I use stainless steel for another important reason.

In my opinion when cooking at medium to high temperatures this is the way to go. On rare occasions I'll use a glass pot to make things like natural healing drinks and other types of teas because food tends to stick to them. However if you know how to use stainless steel pans properly you'll almost never have a problem with food stinking to them, even omelets and fish. It's pretty easy to figure out how to get a stainless steel pan to act like a non-stick pan. Once the pan is heated to a high enough temp you can put your oil or butter in. But be careful because when too hot you'll burn your butter in 3 seconds.

See my website blog page you'll find my "Seven Egg Italian Omelet" recipe where I show you how I made this huge omelet without it sticking. Just visit mariomazzo.com/blog to see it.

So in "my opinion" it's always best to use a stainless steel pan not only for all of the recipes in this book which require use of a pan, but you can use them for just about anything. I prefer them over aluminum all the time. And I also don't want aluminum getting into my food. It's not good for you! Plus many experts say: that traces of aluminum ingested over long periods of time can increase the odds of getting Alzheimer's and other diseases. I don't know about you, but I prefer to keep my mind and memory, thank you.

GLASS & CERAMIC

I love to use glass or ceramic dishes for baking casseroles or lasagna, baked ziti, chicken or eggplant parmesan and other things. But like I said I do not like them on a stovetop because the direct heat will usually cause food to burn or stick on the bottom. Please make sure to use heat resistant glass or baking dishes are made for high temperatures. Do not use serving trays in an oven and make sure they have the proper heat specifications listed on the package when new.

NON-STICK

So the short story to why I don't like non-stick cookware is that for years in the past manufacturers have recommended that you do NOT use them on high heat. What? Okay, then I won't use them at all, thanks for the tip manufacturer. Even though many stores still sell them I have not used them for many years.

Years ago I actually decided to read the warning label that came inside the box of the new non-stick pan I just purchased. It stated not to use this pan on high heat. Why? I have no idea. But a few years after using these types of pans something didn't jive with me about this. In the 1980's when these became popular I was only in my 20's and health wasn't one of my priorities. But a few years later after putting two and two together, I thought maybe I should stop using them due to the warning label alone.

I have no idea why so many celebrity chefs are still using them on TV shows but it's there's probably 2 main reasons that aren't too difficult to figure out. I've even seen lots of YouTube Videos of people using them for deep frying. This should be a big no-no if they are still made of the same ingredients.

Maybe lately the companies improved the quality of the chemicals used to make the non-stick pans, but I doubt that. They are probably still not safe to use at high temperatures and they can also peal and get into your food. So I say no to them. I've heard pet shop owners tell me to throw them in the garbage if I have birds which I used to have, and that if a bird's cage is near the kitchen it could make the bird sick or die. I thought then I am breathing this stuff in too and it all made sense to me. So goodbye non-stick hello stainless steel.

COMMON RECIPE ABBREVIATIONS

° C - Celsius
C - Celsius
C - Centigrade
° F - Fahrenheit
F - Fahrenheit
"- inch or inches
c - cup
doz - dozen
fl oz - fluid ounce
g - gram
gal - gallon
gm - grams
hr - hour or hours
kg – kilogram
L - liter
lb - pound
mil - milliliter
min - minute
mins - minutes
oz - ounce or ounces
pt - pint
qt - quart
sq - square
Tbsp or T - tablespoon
tsp or t - teaspoon
approx. - approximately

MEASUREMENT + CONVERSION GUIDES

RECIPE EQUIVALENTS

ALL MEASUREMENTS ARE ROUNDED OFF

1/2 fl oz = 3 tsp = 1 tbsp = 15 ml
1 fl oz = 2 tbsp = 1/8 cup = 30 ml
2 fl oz = 4 tbsp = 1/4 cup = 60 ml
3 fl oz = 6 tbsp = _____ = 89 ml
4 fl oz = 8 tbsp = 1/2 cup = 118 ml
5 fl oz = 10 tbsp = _____ = 148 ml
6 fl oz = 12 tbsp = 3/4 cup = 178 ml
7 fl oz = 14 tbsp = _____ = 150 ml
8 fl oz = 1/2 pint = 16 tbsp = 1 cup = 236 ml
9 fl oz = _____ = 18 tbsp = ____ = 270 ml
10 fl oz = _____ = 20 tbsp = ____ = 296 ml
16 fl oz = 1/2 quart = 1 pint = 2 cups = 473 ml
32 fl oz = 1 quart = 2 pints = 4 cups = 946 ml
128 fl oz = 1 gallon = 4 quarts = 8 pints = 3.78 liters
1/3 & 2/3 CUP
 1/3 cup = 5.3 tbsp = 2.66 oz = 78 ml
 2/3 cup = 10.65 tbsp = 5.33 oz = 157 ml

CONVERSIONS US to METRIC

U.S. to Metric Capacity

1/4 tsp = 1 ml
1 tsp = 5 ml
1 Tbsp = 15 ml
1/4 cup = 60 ml
1 cup = 240 ml
2 cups (1 pint) = 480 ml
4 cups (1 quart) = 0.96 liter (or 960 ml)
4 quarts (1 gal) = 3.79 liters

U.S. to Metric Weight

1 fluid oz. = 29.6 milliliters
1 fluid oz. = 28.35 grams
1 pound = 454 grams

Metric to U.S. Capacity

1 ml = 1/5 tsp
5 ml = 1 tsp
10 ml = 2 tsp
15 ml = 1/2 fluid oz = Tbsp
30 ml = 1 fluid oz = 2 Tbsp
100 ml = 3.4 fluid oz
240 ml = 1 cup
1 liter = 34 fluid oz
1 liter = 4.2 cups
1 liter = 2.1 pints
1 liter = 1.06 quarts
1 liter = 0.26 gallon

Metric to U.S. Weight

1 gram = 0.035 ounce
100 grams = 3.52 ounces
500 grams = 17.63 ounces
500 grams = 1.10 pounds
1 kilogram = 2.2045 pounds
1 kilogram = 35 ounces

TEMPERATURE CONVERSIONS

Fahrenheit (°F) to Celsius (°C)

0 °F	-17.78 °C
10 °F	-12.22 °C
20 °F	-6.67 °C
30 °F	-1.11 °C
40 °F	4.44 °C
50 °F	10.00 °C
60 °F	15.56 °C
70 °F	21.11 °C
80 °F	26.67 °C
90 °F	32.22 °C
100 °F	37.78 °C
110 °F	43.33 °C
120 °F	48.89 °C
130 °F	54.44 °C
140 °F	60.00 °C
150 °F	65.56 °C
160 °F	71.11 °C
170 °F	76.67 °C
180 °F	82.22 °C
190 °F	87.78 °C
200 °F	93.33 °C
300 °F	148.89 °C
400 °F	204.44 °C
500 °F	260.00 °C
600 °F	315.56 °C
700 °F	371.11 °C
800 °F	426.67 °C
900 °F	482.22 °C
1000 °F	537.78 °C

ITALIAN COOKING 101

The quality and freshness of ingredients used in your recipes is the key factor to make great tasting food. All experienced chefs will agree.

Should you always use the best ingredients for a recipe? Yes! When making Italian food it's important to use good extra virgin olive oil from, Italy, Spain, or even Chile.

Lately I've tried some delicious oil from Chile and this has become my favorite. I don't cook with Extra Virgin Olive Oil (EVOO) at higher temperatures. I mostly use it to drizzle as a topping, or only during the last couple minutes of baking if that type of flavor is called for.

Most well-known television chefs always use EVOO when cooking. They don't teach to use this oil only for low heat or no heat. Why don't they teach these things? I have no idea, and I'm very disappointed that they constantly push for EVOO in all Italian cooking during baking or cooking.

From what I understand, according to the International Olive Council, this oil is "not" to be used at higher temperatures. To give more specific details please do your own research.

Please read about the reasons why this oil is to be used only at lower temperatures in the Olive Oil chapter of this book and on the International Olive Council's website.

Italian cooking is known for fresh herbs and aromatics such as garlic, onions, basil, rosemary, and oregano. Choosing a decent quality salt helps too. Great salts for cooking are, Sea Salt, Himalayan Salt, Celtic Salt and several others. Regular cheap table salt is processed and not recommended.

The most important to remember when making Italian food is that you should never compromise by using inferior tomatoes or cheese. These two ingredients usually make up 80% of the flavor of most Italian dishes. So the better quality of these two, usually equals better food.

I didn't spend countless hours creating this cookbook later learn that Joe Blow Pepperoni Head read this book, made out his shopping list, ran down to the closest store and bought the cheapest flavorless mozzarella cheese, which only saved him a measly $0.65 cents per pound compared to the better brands.

And Joe if you're out there and reading this, I didn't mean to offend you but you probably needed to hear this. Oh, and there's one more thing I should add while I'm on the subject. Please don't buy the cheapest brand of canned tomatoes, especially when there's a buy one get one free sale.

Shopping this way only creates bad habits and will not contribute to better tasting food. Sorry to have to burst your bubble, but your recipe will either be bland, or maybe even suck.

You basically just took a great recipe and screwed it up by trying to save a buck or two. Please don't blame me or this cookbook, or its recipes if you decide to do these things okay? There are no ingredient police watching you to keep you in line. Be passionate in life when creating things, especially the food that you put into your stomach. I like quality ingredients, why shouldn't you? Why shouldn't anyone? You'll find them in most grocery stores unless you live way out in the sticks.

Be a good cook, it's not that difficult, and the power is within your hands. I want to help you to make the most fantastic Italian food possible. Maybe after making these recipes a few times you'll be able to turn out the best tasting Italian food in your entire town and just as good as the great restaurants near you.

So remember, the two most important ingredients to focus on for now are the tomatoes and the cheese. All great Italian chefs know this, it's no secret. These two main ingredients can totally transform your meals into amazing ones. You can learn more about finding quality tomatoes and cheese in the following chapters.

TOMATOES

Always choose tomatoes that are imported from Italy if possible. There's no exception for this and it's extremely important for flavor.

The most popular tomato professional and home chef like to use from Italy are San Marzano Italian tomatoes. We in other countries must buy them in cans that are exported from Italy.

If you can't find those words on the can or jar, try to find some that at least say they have been imported from Italy and you'll have a much better chance of your recipes tasting better. I've used many brands of "Italian" tomatoes that did not say

San Marzano on the can or jar and they were just as delicious. So don't freak out if you can't find tomatoes from that region.

However there are times that you buy a jar or can that states it was imported from Italy and they do not taste so great. So try different brands to see which have the sweetest rich flavor and are less acidic.

TOMATO SAUCE is ALWAYS the STAR to ME

Some call it gravy, others call it marinara, but I just call it red sauce, or tomato sauce. When you taste real homemade sauce, the good kind, you'll remember it.

There are so many tomato sauce recipes out there. Some of them are: Traditional, Bolognaise, Alla Vodka and Ragu or Sunday Sauce. In this book I focus on making straight traditional tomato sauce.

However some of the recipes in this book consist of a meat sauce like the Lasagna with meat sauce. And you will get a great recipe for Penne alla Vodka which has the Vodka sauce. There's even Alfredo sauce in this book so no worries. You should have enough to get you on your way to making some great food with great sauce.

Not only that I teach you how to make a couple types of pizza sauce, you don't have to think that I left that part out of this book.

I haven't included any Ragu or Sunday Sauce recipes because they are really simple to make. And they're so simple that you really don't need much of a recipe.

To make them you just have to cook your favorite meat in a separate frying pan for a few minutes until it's lightly browned on both sides, then take the pieces of meat without the grease or fat, and add them to your pot of sauce at the beginning of its cooking time.

You'll then let all the ingredients simmer together for about 2 to 3 hours or until all of the flavors are married.

Most people making a sauce like this use Italian Sweet Sausage and meatballs combined. You can also use a small piece steak or a slice of brisket. The tomato sauce in my opinion makes the whole recipe.

Whether it's used to make Chicken or Eggplant Parm, or poured over the top of a fresh hot Calzone, it's all delicious to me.

CHEESE

Cheese is also an extremely important ingredient when making Italian food, especially Pizza, Calzone, Lasagna, Chicken Parmesan, Eggplant Parmesan, Fettuccine Alfredo and some other dishes.

Choose the highest quality cheese when making Italian food. This is something that every good Italian chef knows.

There happens to be a pizzeria in Brooklyn that charges about $5.00 for a slice of his delicious pizza. Why so much you ask?

Well, it's because he uses the finest and freshest ingredients. And how do I know this? Not only have I watched online videos of him making a pizza, including a documentary video,

I've personally seen him face to face making pizzas while I was waiting in line for my few slices. I can tell you that his pizza had such a rich cheese taste that I haven't had anywhere else in the world.

His plain cheese pizza that I ordered was so delicious. I saw actually chopping fresh chunks of cheese and bake these pies.

Why is there always a line of people to get his pizza? Because he uses good quality cheese and tomatoes. I'm sure he uses the best flour to make the pizza dough too. But listen, dough can be a little forgiving, but cheese and tomatoes never are and always tell a story.

This guys is ranked usually in the top 4 spots for New York Pizza and I now know why. His pizza has a very rich taste due to the quality of the cheeses he uses.

The main types of cheese used for Italian cooking are usually: Mozzarella, Ricotta, Parmesan and Romano. There are others also but these are the most popular types used for almost every Italian meal you will ever eat. So learn about them.

CHEESE TIPS

When buying Mozzarella cheese always get the "whole milk mozzarella" if available. Why take a chance and play games? The flavor is fuller and superior to the part skim types for sale. I know many people buy part skim and some recipes even call for this type, but the flavor is just not the same.

I highly doubt that you're going to lose much weight or any, if that's your goal. You'll probably never see a true Italian chef use cheese made from skim milk to make traditional Italian main course dishes.

Don't get me wrong part skim isn't that bad but you'll lose some of the flavor. Let your own taste buds be the judge by doing a taste test it's the best way to know and experience the differences.

This is my favorite way to test ingredients. And it's always good to get in a habit of doing this before making food. Tasting various cheeses before making a recipe, especially with Mozzarella cheese will never hurt.

PARMESAN CHEESE

However, you won't have to test Parmigiano-Reggiano or the Pecorino Romano cheese if they're imported from Italy. Those always have a rich consistent taste the same and are delicious.

Pecorino Romano is a very strong tangy cheese though made from sheep's milk. Just please make sure they are "true imports" and not copies from other countries. Most stores sell at least one imported brand of Parmigiano Reggiano or Pecorino Romano from Italy. So you don't have to worry.

I have had some great tasting Parmesan cheese from Uruguay lately. Parmigiano-Reggiano from Italy is my first choice and the Uruguay Parmesan cheese is my second favorite.

I know it's not from Italy but it tastes great. And if there's no Reggiano available I get the Uruguay cheese, or my third choice Grana Padano. Sometimes I like the Grana Padano from Italy. The Grana Padano cheese is called the poor man's Reggiano.

The Uruguay Parmesan definitely beat it hands down the last time I tasted them both back to back at the store. So let's talk about the differences between my two favorites.

The Reggiano Parmesan from Italy has a nuttier sweet taste than the Parmesan from Uruguay.

The Uruguay Parmesan cheese had a saltier taste but not as sweet and no nutty flavor. Both are delicious though and it may even be a good idea to mix together one day just to see how they blend.

Many people mix grated Parmigiano-Reggiano with Romano cheese together but I don't prefer those mixed. I like Romano cheese sometimes but it's a bit too strong for me usually and I really only use it when I make Sicilian Pizza.

MOZZARELLA

When it comes to Mozzarella the best thing to do is to compare it to other Mozzarella cheeses Remember, most stores let you taste a sample of their cheese or meat before you buy them from the deli dept.

Higher end Italian delis and other stores, even whole food type stores will let you sample products especially cheese before buying, so ask a clerk to point you towards the good stuff and ask to taste a few brands.

The best mozzarella and ricotta cheese usually come in 1 pound sealed packages and containers. The Parmesan and Romano usually come in a freshly cut triangle off the round cheese wheel and are usually located in the refrigerated section near the deli.

IMPORTANT for the CHEESE TEST

For those of you that aren't fortunate enough to find a store to let you sample the imported cheese on the spot, you may have to buy a few types and bring them home.

First, you should always buy ingredients and food with the freshest dates you can find. Sometimes the exp. date can vary many months, so look through a couple of packages.

With dairy and cheese this is important.

Fresher is better. There's no need to go crazy buying more than 2 or 3 brands for each taste test. Just make sure to keep an accurate record of the winners and write them down on a piece of paper and develop your own ranking system.

Make sure to not only write down the winners but also the losers, and take good notes for both. Hide the list in a kitchen drawer until the next time you want to do this again so you won't buy the same brands again.

You'll keep this record of tests for the future until you have a clear winner. For the test just bring the cheese home, open them both "at the same time" and then taste them. It's simple, you're done.

FOR OLIVE OIL TOO

Now record everything on paper and save as mentioned above. I do this for everything, especially olive oil, or butter.

I just tested an olive oil imported from Chile (which is currently my favorite) vs. and olive oil from Italy and Chile won easily and blew away all the others I have put it up against it.

It's no wonder that they won awards for their olive oil. To find it, just look for the colorful label. It tasted sweeter and fresher. I even noticed fruity notes in this oil.

Unfortunately the Italian oils had more of a bitter taste. But if you go shopping for an expensive Italian Olive Oil maybe you'll find a better one. Who knows? I'll stick with my new favorite oil for now.

All brands are different so do your homework. It's good to email yourself the results of everything you liked so the next time you're at the store you can just check your email.

You can even perform similar tests with wine and many other things also. Be sure to drink some water in between each sample to reset your taste buds or eat some bread in between.

CHEESE RATINGS & TIPS

Below are some popular store brands of cheese available at most grocery stores. I listed mostly the mozzarella brands because there are so many to choose from.

Look for the best full flavored mozzarella cheese you can find. It's usually much easier to find a decent ricotta quickly.

When making the ricotta cheesecake in this cookbook, common sense will tell you that since Ricotta cheese will be the main ingredient you'll want to get your hands on a good one. You probably figured that out already. I just wanted to give you a heads up before you go out and stock the ingredients in your fridge.

The brands below of Whole Milk Mozzarella are usually delicious and hard to beat, but let your taste buds be the judge. I never buy skim or low fat so they are not listed here.

BRANDS

Mozzarella: Grande, Calabrio, Capiello, Sorrento, Trader Joe's, Whole Foods 365, Polly-O (one of my old time favorites).

Organic Mozzarella: Horizon Organic, Organic Valley.

Mozzarella Buffalo: Try finding a good quality Buffalo cheese. They're at most stores and especially higher end stores like Whole Foods, etc.

Ricotta Regular: Polly-O and Sorrento are two easy to find brands at most stores. They're both easy to locate depending on where you live and are delicious.

Ricotta Organic: Probably any organic ricotta you find in the store should be a high enough quality, but taste-test them at home before deciding to use them in a recipe just to be sure.

Some reviews for the best tasting mozzarella cheese coming from the internet rank Capiello and Trader Joe's brand highly. You might want to add those to the list below the Polly-O.

Remember that if a recipe calls for 1 cup of mozzarella along with two tablespoons of ricotta, then you probably won't need to be as concerned with the small amount of a lesser quality ricotta drastically changing the flavor of that dish.

At least not nearly as much as the mozzarella can. But it's better to stay on the safe side when possible. I usually try to stick with organic cheese or meat if at all possible for health reasons. Especially when the cheese doesn't come from Italy and is made in the USA.

I'm against the added hormones and other things that are feed to these animals. Eating organic meats and cheese is way up there on the list if you're going to choose anything organic to eat. I do notice a difference in the flavor of the organic meat and dairy products.

You might also. But once again, always look for Imported Italian Cheese when making Italian food. Some dairy tips:

Try experimenting and tasting some organic cheeses, sour creams, yogurts and other milk products available. You may be pleasantly surprised and not go back the regular stuff.

Maybe you won't notice much of a difference in flavor but at least you're probably getting a healthier product. I've had organic cheese, organic yogurts, and organic sour cream that were fantastico!

I'm not familiar with too many brands especially brands from Europe or the UK so please do your research if you can't find these brands in your local store.

FLOUR

The cup measurements for 1 pound of flour will vary, depending on the type of flour used.

Here's an example of a few types below.

1 pound of all-purpose flour = approx. 3 + 1/3 cups
1 pound of cake flour = approx. 4 + 1/2 cups
1 pound pastry flour = approx. 4 + 1/4 cups
1 pound whole wheat flour = approx. 3 + 1/3 cups

YEAST

When making fresh bread, pizzas, a calzones or cakes you'll need some yeast. I've chosen 3 of the most popular yeast types on the following pages to give you a crash course on yeast.

If you're beginner at baking I highly suggest you watch this 4 minute video from the King Arthur Flour Company. It's an excellent video and will educate you in detail on 4 or 5 types of yeast used for baking.

If you bought this book in paperback version and are not able to click on the clickable link below you can just go to YouTube and type the words below into the search bar and it should come up as the first result.

"Yeast 101 by How2Heros"

Here is the clickable link for digital book readers youtube.com/watch?v=P4NO7xBHl7s

INSTANT DRY YEAST

This yeast is much easier to work with and has a finer texture. It can be mixed right into dry ingredients. It's a dry yeast which is made in a process similar to making active dry yeast but is dried quicker, so it dissolves faster and activates rapidly.

It does NOT have to be proofed first meaning that you don't have to add it to water first. This means it can be mixed directly into the dry ingredients and achieves the same result.

It's usually the preferred choice of yeast for most home bakers

However, although this yeast doesn't need to be proofed first, is better to do that anyway just to ensure the yeast hasn't gone bad before using it.

This will help you to avoid a recipe disaster of not having your bread, pizza, cake or calzone rise unless you like to gamble.

It only takes about 10 or 15 minutes to see if the yeast is still good by proofing anyway.

To do this use a little water that is equal to your body temperature and mix it with a sprinkle of sugar. If it foams or bubbles within 15 minutes it's good to use in the recipe.

Just make sure to measure the water you used to count it towards the recipe.

RAPID RISE or QUICK RISE INSTANT YEAST

This one is also a favorite, among many bakers at home. However, this type of yeast has extra enzymes or other additives to help the dough rise faster. The added benefit provided by using this yeast is that it can bypass the first rise of the dough, so you can form your loaves of bread or pizza immediately after kneading.

This yeast also does not have to be proofed with water before making your dough. Remember that when using this yeast though you'll still need to wait usually between 10 to 30 minutes before baking.
For example when making a Sicilian pizza, after you've formed the dough inside the pan let it rise and double in size before baking the pizza or adding your layers of the sauce and cheese. This way the dough will puff up before baking to give your Sicilian pie an airy texture which is important for this type of pizza.

ACTIVE DRY YEAST

This yeast needs to be dissolved and proofed in approx. 1 cup of lukewarm water before using it. It has larger granules similar to cornmeal and needs to be proofed since it's a living organism, and is dormant until proofed.

When proofing this yeast, it's usually done in water temperatures of between 95–100 degrees Fahrenheit. You'll be able to see if the yeast is good or bad before using it in your recipe. This is done by letting it sit for about 10 minutes to see if it starts to bubble or foam a little. If it does then its good, if not it's bad so don't use it, but start over with another yeast. This not only activates the yeast but also is the way to check it before using it.

Please take note that if the water you're using is too hot or too cold you can kill the yeast so test the water by touching it with your finger before adding the yeast and try to get the water as close to your body temperature as possible. After adding the yeast to water, you'll notice that after 10 to 20 minutes it start foaming which means it has proofed. At this point it's okay to wait a few more minutes before adding the yeast water to your recipe.

Always use a little less water than your recipe calls for or the exact amount but never more. You can always add more water later to the recipe to make up for the difference. Don't forget this. Experienced bakers prefer using this active dry yeast which requires proofing or fresh refrigerated yeasts. This yeast is usually sold in individual small packets or small jars.

WHICH YEAST SHOULD YOU USE?

That depends on what you're baking and how much waiting you don't mind doing while the dough is rising. My suggestion for what it's worth is that you start off with either the Rapid Rise Instant Yeast or the Instant Dry Yeast. Instant yeasts are easier and more convenient to work with.

You can experiment with different types of yeast from time to time and see which you prefer using. You might notice a slight difference in the flavor of the finished product. So why not experiment?

Some professional bakers only use Active Dry Yeast because they prefer the flavor and end result. There may be minor difference that you might not even notice. Just remember before buying your yeast know how to use it. To learn more about yeast or anything relating to food, it's always recommended to do a little research because the little bit you learn can make or break your recipe.

To make your baking life easier here's a link King Arthur Flour's website. They specialize in flour and have various types. They offer plenty of yeast information on their page.
See the website below.
kingarthurflour.com/learn/yeast.html

SUGAR & SALT

SUGAR

Organic sugar is used in the kitchen to replace regular processed sugar. It's much healthier for you. I'm not an organic fanatic, but I believe that certain ingredients should always be organic and sugar is one of them.

You or may not notice a difference in the flavor but at least you're not eating another processed ingredient. Regular processed sugar used chemicals to make it a bright white color.

It's most likely full of toxins so many health experts suggest using organic sugar, honey or other natural sweeteners that are not heavily processed.

Brown sugar isn't processed the same way that the white is and is more natural. It has a richer flavor but you don't want to add brown sugar to a recipe randomly unless it calls for it because it can change the flavor.

SALT

Salt is one of my favorite ingredients. It's not only packed with many minerals but it tastes great. Just don't use too much of it when cooking.

Less is better. You can always add more with the salt shaker on the table to your plate of food while eating.

I avoid regular table salt that's processed with chemicals. Although this salt has iodine added to it, which is an important mineral for your body I'd still rather use sea salt or Himalayan salt. I take an iodine supplement since I don't use iodized salt since it's difficult to get it in food.

There are many types of salt, probably dozens of them. They taste great and all have a different flavor. Try them all and stick with the ones you like best.

Himalayan salt can be a little grainier and usually takes longer to break down but is supposed to be one of the healthiest regardless of what scam watchdogs say.

It's probably better to use sea salt in recipes and the pink salt on the table to season your food with.

I use the pink salt in recipes too though and everything seems to come out fine without getting too grainy.

There are many other types of salt that you can buy and are fun to experiment with. Taste them all and see which you prefer for different recipes.

OLIVE OIL

There are so many grades and types of olive oil. I will discuss the 4 most popular types you can buy at most stores. Since olive oil is frequently used for Italian cooking just remember this one thing.

Olive oil from Italy, Spain, Greece, California and now Chile are used in homes and restaurants worldwide.

When you're at the store, try selecting a great tasting olive oil. It's important. The three main types that most stores stock are: Extra-Virgin, Virgin, or Pure Olive Oil, and Light Olive Oil.

Most experts say that Extra virgin is of higher quality and tastes better, and although this is true it can frequently be on the bitter side. So choose your extra virgin or virgin oil carefully.

The other types of olive oil have less flavor, but can be heated to higher temperatures. This is not the case with the two virgin types.

They are more delicate and should be used mainly as a dressing or while recipes are cooked at lower temperatures. You will not normally hear about this from TV cooking shows, but this is the first thing any Italian chef should teach others.

So when lightly pan frying some chicken parmesan or eggplant parmesan you may want to use regular olive oil or a sunflower oil, which tend to break down less under heat as opposed to virgin or extra virgin olive oil.

Using extra virgin olive oil to fry foods in is not in your best interest for two reasons. First it breaks down faster under higher heat plus it has a stronger or peppery taste.

So let your taste buds be your judge and always taste the olive oil before using it. I usually only use it in a pan at low temperatures, like for example to sizzle some garlic for 20 seconds in order to transfer the flavor of the garlic into the oil.

With olive oil, there are many factors to consider, purity, acidity, and other things.
On the following pages I explain some basics about olive oil to help you get you cooking quickly.

EXTRA VIRGIN OLIVE OIL aka (EVOO)

EVOO is from the first press of the olives and has more flavor than the rest of the grades. It usually has fruity or peppery notes and aromas. Some brands can tend to be on the bitter side so choose your brand carefully.

This oil is great to pour over your salad or even drizzled over a pizza during the last minute its baking or after you take it out of the oven, which adds a nice touch of flavor.

Some chefs don't use it for cooking at medium to high temperatures because they know it should be used at lower cooking temps. See the International Olive Oil Council website to learn more.

I love pouring some into a small dipping bowl while eating so I can dip a piece of freshly baked bread into it. This oil has the highest standards in quality and processing.

VIRGIN OLIVE OIL

This oil has a milder flavor than the extra virgin grade and tends to be less bitter, but is also delicious. You must still taste many brands to see which you prefer.

Although this oil isn't as popular as the extra virgin oil there are some stores that carry it. The extra virgin grade is usually the way to go, but you may find a great tasting virgin oil sometimes. If you do there's nothing wrong with buying that type. Both virgin grades extra and regular have very high standard of production and processing.

PURE OLIVE OIL aka OLIVE OIL

Pure olive oil also known as regular olive oil usually has a lot less flavor, which is the preferred oil to cook with when cooking between medium to high temperatures.

This oil won't add the strong flavors that the others carry to your food and shouldn't break down while cooking at higher temperatures nearly as easy.

There can still be a slight detectable aroma in this oil since it's usually a blend of virgin oil and the remaining oil in the olives which hasn't been pressed out yet.

Pure olive oil and olive oil are both the same so don't let these names confuse you. This oil is also considered "regular" olive oil, and usually a blend of virgin olive oil and refined olive oil.

It's lighter in color than its two virgin sister oils. The bad news about this oil is that in the manufacturing process heat, chemicals, or both are used. So if you're trying to live a healthy lifestyle then you may want to remember this the next time you go shopping.

LIGHT OLIVE OIL aka MILD OLIVE OIL

Light olive oil is similar to pure or regular olive oil. However, this oil is highly refined and is usually created by adding an even lesser quality virgin oil than they would normally use as with the pure olive oil.

It's not less in calories or fat so don't let the name fool you. It has almost the identical stuff that the pure olive oil has, but it's more refined which can make this a better cooking oil at even higher temperatures.

I personally do not use this type of oil. I've used EVOO, virgin, or pure. I prefer EVOO for a dressing, dipping or drizzling over cooked food.

For cooking or stir frying I normally use sunflower oil or butter.

Light olive oil is lighter in color (usually yellow), lighter in flavor, and usually very little or no aroma. It also goes by the name cooking oil, because of its neutral taste and higher smoke point.

It can be used for baking, sautéing, grilling, and even higher temperature frying.

INTERNATIONAL OLIVE OIL COUNCIL DEFINITIONS

On the website of International Olive Council they've got lots of great info. A definition they give regarding Virgin Olive Oil for example goes something like this.

It is the oil produced from the fruit of the olive tree has only been processed and extracted by mechanical or other ways that will not cause alteration or deterioration to the oil.

Neither have heat, solvents, chemical interaction, or any form of radiation been used in the process of producing this oil including the use of microwaves!

So to me this is the way to go when wanting to add flavor to your meals but don't cook with it. And the council states on their website that it's not advised to cook with this oil at higher temperatures.

MY OPINION on OLIVE OIL

So if you want my two cents about olive oil here it is. You should always try to find a sweet tasting virgin or extra-virgin olive oil because both follow a high standard of quality during the manufacturing process!

When shopping, I normally choose extra virgin olive oil. I bring it home and keep it away from heat and light. I keep the cap closed tightly and it lasts about a month or two because it's used as a condiment for flavor or even a natural remedy instead of medicine. I like the fact that this oil hasn't been subjected to any form of treatment other than regular things like expeller pressure, washing, and filtration in the process of making it, along with other things that help to ensure and not compromise its safety, quality and integrity.

However, there is one catch. Just to add a little confusion to your life I should tell you that, The International Olive Oil Institute recommends using pure olive oil, and not the virgin grade, when you're frying since the flavor and integrity of virgin olive oils can break down at higher temperatures. This can cause health issues and also create a bitter tasting oil in your recipes. So now you have lots to think about. So be careful about the type of oil you use, and for which purpose.

OLIVE OIL TAKEAWAY

1. If you want to stay healthy try to do as little frying as possible since oils break down at higher temps. But as for lower temp cooking or sautéing using delicate oils shouldn't be a problem.

2. Using a sweet, mild tasting virgin or extra virgin olive oil is a good choice for salads or dipping, but not most cooking.

3. When cooking with oil it's best to use a type or grade that have higher smoke points. You can look up various oils and smoke points online to see which you prefer to use for medium or high temps.

4. When making eggplant or chicken parmesan, which both require shallow pan frying, keep the heat on medium and use higher smoke point oils.

For health reasons you may want to keep the pieces thinly sliced so they cook faster, which will require less cooking time, meaning less oil breakdown. Logically and theoretically this should help the oil to keep its integrity.

5. Another option for cooking at high temps are using coconut oil but it has a sweet taste and doesn't usually go well with Italian food ingredients but it has a very high smoke point. I prefer sunflower or safflower oil for Italian or most recipes.

6. Cooking with oils such as sunflower or safflower, usually have decent high smoke points and offer a mild taste which is what you want. You don't usually want your oil to flavor the food too much while it's cooking.

You should be careful when heating up oils as they can cause many health issues and have been known to cause cancer when used at extreme temperatures like when deep frying for example.

Foods that are totally submerged in a very hot oil like when making French fries for example can cause the oil to break down. This is a type of food you wouldn't want to eat frequently.

7. There's no need to be paranoid, just be a little careful. Eating fried foods cooked in a deep fryer a few times per week is not the wisest thing to do if you care about staying healthy or getting well.

I'm not a doctor so don't take my word for it but do your own research. I've listened to many natural doctors over the years and they all say the same thing about avoid fried foods and reduce the risk cancer getting out of control in your body.

8. When baking things like a Sicilian pizza which requires extended baking time, l prefer using sunflower oil lately in the dough recipe instead of olive oil.

9. Your decisions are your own of course. I just wanted to provide some options for you and try to always keep the original recipe ingredients intact without changing them. So feel free to substitute the oils.

PASTA TYPES & COOKING TIMES

Cooking times can greatly vary according to type of pasta and other variables. This list should give you a general idea of the cooking times for pastas. The range of numbers used below are for minutes.

DRIED PASTA LIST

Acini de pepe 4-6
Angel Hair 4-6
Capellini 4-6
Egg noodles (regular) 8-10
Egg noodles (extra wide) 10-12
Elbow macaroni 8-10
Farfalle 13-15
Fettuccine 11-13
Fusilli 11-13
Japanese curly noodles 4-5
Lasagna noodles 12-15
Linguine 9-13
Mafalda 8-10
Manicotti 10-12
Mostaccioli 12-14
Penne 9-13
Rigatoni 12-15
Rosamarina or Orzo 8-10
Rotelle 10-12
Rotini 8-10
Shells (Small and Medium) 9-11
Shells (Jumbo) 12-15
Soba noodles 6-7
Spaghetti 8-10
Vermicelli 5-7
Wagon wheel 10-12
Ziti 14-15

REFRIGERATED PACKAGED or FRESH PASTA

Angel Hair 1-2
Capellini 1-2
Linguine 1-2
Farfalle 2-3
Ravioli 6-8
Fettuccine 1-2
Tortellini 8-10
Lasagna 2-3

DELICIOUS PASTA TIPS

The Pasta

For the tastiest pasta use "Durum Wheat" Italian pasta. I'm not saying to buy the brown whole wheat pasta. That's not what I'm talking about at all. Also, try not to use pasta that has been fortified if other choices are available at the store when shopping.

The Water

As your water starts to boil add some salt. Sea salt is preferred. Usually 1 or 2 tablespoons are sufficient but it really depends on how much water you are using. The general rule is approx. 1 tablespoon for each quart or liter (approx. 32 oz water). I use about half this amount and the pasta tastes salty enough for me.

The boiling water should taste salty like the ocean. Add a couple of tablespoons of Semolina flour to the boiling water if you have any. Now add your pasta. Cook until al dente or a little longer.

Removing and Rinsing the Pasta

To Rinse or Not to Rinse?

You have many options. Many pros say don't rinse. I say why not? Yeah, yeah I know the reasons many say don't rinse. I know that the idea of not rinsing is to help the sauce stick to the pasta better and keep the salty flavor. I say whatever floats your boat…

The most important thing is to eat delicious pasta and make the people your feeding happy, especially yourself when cooking for one or two.

I have tried both ways and I prefer rinsing 90% of the time for various reasons. Sorry celebrity chefs.

On occasion I won't rinse pasta for certain dishes like Fettuccini Alfredo, and even then it's okay to rinse the pasta a little as long as you drip dry or drain it well when it's done or your sauce will be watery, or soupy, and that's the worst.

Since we're on the subject of Fettuccine Alfredo, to rinse pasta, drain it very well, shake all of the water out with your hands, and then throw it into the pan containing the hot Alfredo sauce for a minute or two before serving. This should coat it well enough and any water should evaporate in 1 minute over a low heat.

Plus by doing this the pasta won't get too sticky and glue like. This is the main reason I usually like to rinse pasta.

The advantages of rinsing outweigh the disadvantages in my mind. I'll just discuss the advantages here in case you're not experienced in the kitchen. For starters, after the pasta is rinsed you can walk away for a while and resume cooking or heating it whenever you like.

Go walk the dog, or take out the trash and resume cooking without the threat of it getting too soft or sticky by getting it out of that hot water.

Next, your pasta will be perfectly cooked and not threaten the consistency of the sauce. I don't like gooey thick starchy sauce unless I'm making macaroni and cheese. Once the starch is rinsed off the pasta this will also safeguard your sauce from getting too thick or starchy.

Both are good ways to cook pasta but not rinsing requires more skills and you have to work quickly. You'll also have to eat quickly or your meal will get cold.

After it gets cold it's a bad idea to take non rinsed pasta and heat it up again. The hot starch coating it normally makes it too soft and I don't like my pasta too soft. I prefer it either cooked al dente or perfect, but never overcooked or gooey.

Also I like the option of taking the left over rinsed "un-eaten" pasta that hasn't touched the sauce and keep it in the fridge and use it later in the week. I can use it later with whatever sauce I want, to eat it with, but I frequently I use it for making Lo Mein. It only takes me about 15 minutes to prepare everything for the Lo Mein if I already have some spaghetti cooked and don't have to mess with that part.

If that's not your thing, you can mix it with butter and garlic and a touch of olive oil like I also do on occasions. Or make my Dad's Old Fashioned Favorite, Spaghetti with Ketchup and Butter. Yes I know you think that sounds gross, but after acquiring a taste for it, it's not that bad. My point is that there are lots of things you can do with day old left over pasta.

Oh yeah, almost forgot about Mom's wide noodle pasta baked with butter, cottage cheese and cinnamon. A little tip that I can offer is to use your hands is good to all the starch off. And always taste your pasta to see if it's cooked enough before dumping out all of the hot water from the pot in case you'd like to throw it back in for a few seconds to heat up again.

More Technical Stuff + Tips

Rinsing pasta has two main purposes: one will stop the cooking process from the contact with the cold water which helps it to turn out perfect every time. The second will get rid of the sticky starch and keep it from sticking together.

You may ask what if the pasta sit in the cold water and it gets too cold to eat, then what? Simple, heat it up for a minute using the same hot water left in the pot when you are ready to eat.

I have a good system. Take only as much as you'll eat for that meal and throw it back into the hot water. When you're ready to eat more. You do not have to rinse it again if it only heats up in the water for a minute or two. This is another reason I like to make my pasta al dente. Then I can heat up a second time without it getting too cooked!

Refrigerate the cooked rinsed naked pasta, and use the next time with whatever sauce you like. When saving extra un-eaten cooked and rinsed pasta it should stay fresh in the fridge for about 3 or 4 days.

My rule of thumb is cooked foods including dairy get eaten within 2 or 3 days usually.

Cooked meats, beans, and protein 2 days.

Pasta can probably sit for 4 or 5 days in a cold refrigerator.

Be creative and try cooking your pasta different ways to see which is best for you.

No Rinse Tips

Remove all of the pasta immediately when done cooking into a large serving bowl using a fork or pasta scooper. To do this follow the 3 steps.

1. Lift the pasta up with fork or pasta scooper over the pot for a few seconds letting 99% of the water drip off.

2. Either place it immediately into the sauce pot and mix or into an empty large serving bowl and mix with some of the sauce from the sauce pot or coat it with olive oil or butter so it won't t stick together.

3. Serve and eat before it cools.

Short Rinse Tips

Usually the pasta is sticky and will stick together if you don't work quickly after removing it from the pot, especially when not rinsing. One option I like to use is a very short rinse in cold water for about 10 seconds.

1. I throw all the pasta into a clean purified cold water bath in a mixing bowl or a pot.

2. Using my hands I vigorously shake the pasta for about 5 seconds.

3. I then remove the pasta immediately from the water and let all the water drain off by putting it into a colander or just hold it up in the air for a few seconds with a pasta fork. This also helps it to stop cooking.

4. Then you can then place the pasta into a dry bowl or a bowl that has been coated with oil.

5. Toss the pasta around for 5 seconds with forks for clean hands. You only need just a small amount of oil to keep it from sticking. A little oil goes a long way.

When making pasta with a white cream sauce like Alfredo you may skip rinsing it, but just make sure to eat it quickly before it gets sticky and gooey.

Long Rinse Tips

If you're making a lot of pasta and think you may have some left over, then do a longer rinse for a couple of minutes. This helps remove most of the outside sticky starch. I prefer doing this for many reasons. This way I can have leftover pasta and heat up it again for 2 minutes in hot water as mentioned before.

1. Dump the pasta into a colander placed inside the sink.

2. Run cold water over it while using a fork or your hands to toss it. Be careful not to burn your hands its very hot and you need to cool it under very cold running water for 30 seconds before putting your hands in.

3. Continue rinsing and use your fingers to scrub it together.

4. When done you can place it into a clean water bath.

5. For the water bath, use large clean pot or bowl half full of purified cold water to rinse off the tap water.

6. Drain well, it's ready to either be eaten cold, warmed up in hot water for a minute, or stored in the fridge.

7. Heat up the portions that you are ready to eat in a pot containing 2 inches of hot water and toss and mix for a minute or two. Drain but <u>don't</u> rinse again.

8. You can now place the clean rinsed pasta directly into the sauce or pour sauce on top of it.

9. Serve and eat before it gets cold.

You can also serve the pasta cold and eat with olive oil and lemon or pesto sauce. See the pesto sauce recipe.

Serving Pasta with Olive Oil

1. Place approx.1/4 cup or 4 TBSP of virgin or extra virgin olive oil into a very large serving bowl before adding the pasta. Flavor the oil with a pinch or two of your favorite seasonings or just a pinch of salt. Some examples of seasonings are: salt, pepper, parsley, fresh parmesan cheese, garlic powder, or anything else that you like

2. Before adding the pasta to the bowl with the olive oil, pick it up with tongs, holding it over the pot to drain off all the excess water.

3. Drop pasta directly into bowl with olive oil. Mix by use the tongs for forks picking it up from the bottom a few times to coat the pasta evenly with the oil.

Serving Pasta with Red Sauce

Use the same technique as in serving pasta with olive oil above but instead of using olive oil in the bowl use some red sauce. Don't use too much sauce though because you'll want to save lots of sauce for pouring on top of your pasta.

This is just to coat the pasta to keep it from sticking if you're not going to rinse it. You can use this technique with rinsed pasta also to give it a little color and flavor, before plating it. Then plate it and pour the correct amount of sauce on top for each person's pasta.

Now add any additional seasonings such as fresh cheese or a pinch of something else that you like over the pasta after it's on your personal plate now so that everyone can enjoy it the way that like.

Serving Pasta with White Sauce

Use the same technique as used with the red sauce. Just place the white sauce in instead on the bottom of the bowl first then mix and toss it the same way.

The same basic directions go for white sauce as with the red sauce except this sauce doesn't usually need any extra toppings and it should be perfect with all of the parmesan cheese you just added to the pan for this sauce recipe.

Tips for Eating Pasta for Tomato Sauce Lovers

You're the boss of the food on your own plate so use whichever toppings you love, but if you love tons of tomato sauce the way I do then here are a couple of tips, to prevent all the sauce from disappearing by being absorbed into your pasta. After all the sauce is #1 and the pasta is just a way to eat it right?

Tip # 1 - If mixing the sauce into the pasta before plating it, leave at least half of sauce still in the pot or at least a few tablespoons to pour onto the pasta as a topping but "do not" mix it in so it will stay wet!

Tip # 2 - First, put the pasta on the plate without any sauce, then pour all of the sauce on top. Try not mixing it too much, and each bite will have enough wet sauce without it being absorbed into the pasta. This is my favorite way to eat pasta with red sauce. I like my pasta wet and not too dry with plenty of sauce with each bite.

TOMATO SAUCE TIPS

1. Always add a good sea salt to your tomatoes when making sauce. A little at a time though, don't over salt them because you can add salt when it's finished cooking.

2. Check the sauce after about 45 minutes to check its acidity level. If it's too bitter you can add a few pinches of sugar or some more salt. Just don't over salt it.

3. When buying canned tomatoes try to buy cans stating that the tomatoes were grown in and imported from Italy. Usually you'll see those words on the back of cans in small print.

4. When making tomato sauce, try to use San Marzano canned tomato products if you can find them.

5. Tomatoes grown in the San Marzano region of Italy make the tastiest red sauce, and companies are proud to show the words "San Marzano region of Italy" on the can.

6. The way to choose a good can or jar of tomatoes is this: (1) The San Marzano region of Italy is preferred. (2) The next best location is anywhere in Italy usually. (3) Otherwise taste various brands.

7. To make sauce from scratch use canned tomatoes that are: whole pealed, crushed and pealed, puree, and paste. These are all good but don't use paste by itself, only a little is used time to thicken and make the sauce rich. So only 4 to 8 tablespoons are generally used per pot of sauce.

8. When making a recipe you may be tempted to save time by using store bought or pre-made sauce. Don't do it unless you find a place that makes fresh homemade sauce every day or two and bottles it themselves.

9. Double the amount of tomato sauce a recipe calls for, so you'll have some extra for the week or you can freeze it or a couple of months. .If refrigerating it usually lasts about 7 days before getting moldy.

10. When making a recipe that calls for tomato sauce, have your tomato sauce cooked and heated so it's already made before preparing the rest of the recipe. Some examples of dishes you'll need sauce ready for are chicken parmesan, eggplant parmesan, lasagna, baked ziti and some others.

11. If buying pre made sauce make sure the sauce you buy is super high quality. Some stores like Whole Foods sometimes sell freshly made tomato and sometimes Alfredo sauce in the deli area. I've had both before and they tasted pretty good.

12. Tomato puree products from Italy are great. They come in cans or jars. I've found a few brands in jars that are delicious. The reason I love puree is that it saves lots of time and doesn't have any seeds. I really don't like seeds in sauce they are bitter and I don't like chewing on therm.

Plus they are a real pain to remove wasting valuable time. So puree that is raw and uncooked in a jar is a great way to make sauce. It was even be mixed in a 50-/50 ratio with canned peeled tomatoes for your sauce. It has a nice thick consistency. I'm speaking of puree not paste.

13. When making tomato sauce here's a few steps to help you create some delicious sauce: Open the can or jar. Cut the green hard pieces off the tops of the tomatoes where the stem used to connect.

Cut the tomatoes in quarters looking for seeds to remove with a small spoon. When removing the seeds it's perfectly okay to remove the thick gel like substance the seeds are wrapped in.

Crush the tomatoes with your washed clean hands for about a minute over a bowl and place them in the bowl when finished, you can use a hand blender for about 30 seconds but hands are preferred.

The goal is to break them down in size before cooking. I prefer to squeeze them by hand instead of using the hand blender because the hand blender is a little overkill. You don't need to liquefy them because cooking them will do that for you.

14. If buying puree you'll save the couple steps above. I think you'll probably agree that buying puree is the easiest way to make sauce quickly, and if you're in a hurry then go for it, unless of course you'd like some larger tomato chunks in your sauce which tend to be even tastier. I prefer using the puree for pizza sauce.

15. You can add a small 5 to 6 ounce can of tomato paste to your sauce recipe if you'd like for a little rich and nice flavor. But add about 4 ounces of water with it also.

16. When making homemade tomato sauce you may want to keep an eye on it every 20 minutes. Just take off the cover, give it a good stir on the bottom. This will prevent sticking and burning. You can also add 1 or 2 ounces of water every 30 minutes or whenever you see it's getting too thick, especially if you added paste.

17. Keep the sauce pot covered when making tomato sauce otherwise it will evaporate too quickly and get too thick and burn on the bottom. Plus it always spatters all over the kitchen and your clothes.

18. Always cook your tomato sauce on the lowest heat setting possible.

19. Taste your sauce every 30 minutes. If you do this you'll know when it's done. I know the Italian Grandmas (Nonnas) in the past used to cook their sauce for at least 2 or 3 hours on a low simmer, but to me usually 70 to 90 minutes seems to be plenty of time for the sauce to develop a rich flavor. It's all about what you prefer, and it's your kitchen so do what makes you the happiest!

SUPER SAUCE TIPS

After the sauce has been cooking for about 40 minutes don't be afraid to turn off the heat for 10 minutes and then back on for 10 minutes. Doing this enables you to cook the sauce at super low temperatures and I have found that this gives me a super sauce.

This is my custom low setting. It's a lot more work running back and forth and takes a little more time but if you are already near the kitchen and not taking a nap then it shouldn't make that much of a difference. Just don't forget to turn it back on a couple times per hour for 15 minutes each time.

I use this cooking technique when I see the sauce bubbling like crazy and I don't want it drying up to fast because it will stay very hot for a while and continue to cook even with the heat off.

Just make sure to leave the pot covered for it will get too cool. So if you don't mind babysitting the sauce a little then this little tip may produce some great tasting sauce for you.

Remember that it's difficult to ruin tomato sauce if you take care of it while it's cooking. It can tend to get a dry. So always add a little water to it every now and then while it's simmering away and give it plenty of good stirs while it cooks.

THE RECIPES

Start on the Next Page

Enjoy!

INSALATA CAPRESE (Caprese Salad)

The Proper name: "Insalata Caprese" aka Salad of Capri

ORIGIN

A small island named Capri off the coast of Italy about 3 miles from Sorrento. This simple little treat could be the next hit at your party. If you're not so familiar with Italian food, you may not know the name of this popular salad. You've probably seen it on tables at many restaurants or may have ordered it without knowing its real name.

This tasty snack is one of my favorites and millions of others happen to like it too. Some order it as a salad, others order it as an appetizer but what matters most is that you eat it. The tomatoes and cheese are the stars. A classic Caprese salad served in Italy doesn't have vinegar, but in the good old USA we usually serve this with a Balsamic vinegar reduction drizzled over it which is delicious.

Since this is an Italian-American cookbook, I'll go ahead and give you the American version of this great snack. It's normally difficult for me to put anything else on a fresh tomato besides salt but I don't mind adding cheese balsamic vinegar at all!

INGREDIENTS

14 to 16 oz fresh Buffalo Mozzarella cheese or high quality soft fresh delicious Mozzarella cheese
2 or 3 medium vine ripened tomatoes, at room temperature (organic preferred)
4 TBSP sweet virgin olive oil (organic preferred)
1 oz Balsamic vinegar (organic preferred). Only 1 ounce is required if not making reduction sauce.
8 oz Balsamic vinegar (organic preferred) If choosing to make the reduction sauce.
2 tsp white sugar (organic preferred)
2 pinches sea salt
15 fresh whole basil leaves, rinsed (organic preferred)

Use Only the Best Ingredients for this Salad

When making this special treat use the finest ingredients you can get your hands on for the boldest flavors. You'll want sweet vine ripened tomatoes and a high quality Mozzarella cheese or Buffalo Mozzarella which is preferred. An organic Beefsteak tomato or Italian Plum tomato should both be delicious and are my favorites. A couple of fresh basil leaves won't hurt either.

DIRECTIONS (Balsamic Reduction)

1. Pour about 8 oz Balsamic vinegar into a small stainless steel or ceramic sauce pot. Don't use non-stick pots or pans for this recipe.
2. Heat on low to medium heat and stir frequently.
3. After about 5 minutes or the vinegar has reduced by about half add the sugar. Continue stirring.
4. After 5 more minutes check and taste the liquid with a teaspoon to see if it's lost most of the bitterness and thickens slightly. But don't cook too long or it will burn and you'll have to start over.
5. When it tastes less bitter, becomes a little thicker and develops a sweeter taste, it is probably a good idea to turn the heat off, but continue stirring. And let it sit in the pan for about a minute just to cool for a second. This sauce should reduce to about half its original volume, somewhere in between 3 to 6 ounces.
6. Pour into a small glass cup or directly onto your salad. If getting too thick a few drops of water can be mixed into the syrup to thin it out a little.

DIRECTIONS (Assembling the Salad)

1. Keep the cheese cold in the refrigerator until ready to slice it.

2. Slice tomato to about 1/4 inch thick or a little thinner.

3. Gently poke out most of the tomato seeds with the tip of a sharp knife (nobody likes crunching on bitter tomato seeds).

4. Place tomato decoratively on a plate, in a line or a circle.

5. Sprinkle a couple pinches of salt evenly on the tomato.

6. Slice cheese to about 1/4 inch thick or thinner and place it between each tomato slice or on top of each slice.

7. Tuck a fresh basil leaf in between the tomato and cheese or on top of the cheese. The basil isn't required. It can be used as a garnish or add a little extra flavor.

8. Drizzle, a few spoons of olive oil on top.

9. Drizzle, a few spoons of the "Balsamic vinegar reduction sauce" as a final touch. If using plain straight Balsamic vinegar and not the reduction use only 1 or 2 tablespoons.

NOTES

When making the Balsamic sauce, please note that when heating up vinegar it will probably stink up the whole house.

That's what vinegar does when cooking it. So either open windows in the kitchen or close the kitchen door, or you'll have to deal with the smell. It's very strong.

You have an option of not making the reduction sauce. Instead you can just but sweeten some regular Balsamic vinegar with few pinches of sugar and mix it well.

The sugar will take some of the bite out of the vinegar and you'll still end out with a great recipe, but the reduction sauce is what most people prefer. It's thicker and sweeter.

I like switching off between them both and can go either way. When using the uncooked vinegar just use much less on your food because it's stronger tasting and goes a long way.

About two tablespoons should be all that you need for this recipe.

TOMATO SAUCE RECIPES
5 MINUTE FRESH TOMATO SAUCE

Serves: 2 or 3
Cooks in: 5 mins
Level: Super Easy

Why You May Want This Sauce!

Are you in a hurry to get some tomato sauce cooked fast? Then you might like this simple fast recipe, especially if you need to have sauce on the table in 10 minutes flat.

No need to open some old jar of sauce. Now this sauce won't be as rich as a sauce that has simmered longer on the stove, but if you decide to let it simmer a few more minutes I won't tell anyone.

INGREDIENTS

Two tablespoons of olive oil
1 clove of fresh garlic (minced)
(1) Can Italian Peeled Tomatoes (between15 - 28 oz)
15 ounces of tomato puree
2 or 3 pinches of sea salt
1 pinch of oregano
Option: 1 fresh basil leaf torn in half

DIRECTIONS

1. Mince the garlic
2. Crush the canned tomatoes by hand for 30 seconds or use peeled crushed tomatoes. They must be imported from Italy otherwise super delicious.
3. Using a stainless steel pan, on low heat add 1 tablespoon of fresh olive oil.
4. Add garlic to the oil and stir for 10 seconds and watch it sizzle in the oil.
5. Add the crushed tomatoes and the puree liquid, then stir for 30 seconds.
6. Sprinkle a few pinches of sea salt and oregano with the basil leaf.
7. Cook on medium heat for about 5 minutes or longer, stirring frequently. Allow ingredients to blend.

It's done. You've just made a miraculous and delicious emergency tomato sauce. Remember that the longer you cook the sauce it tends to taste better, so to let it sit a few extra minutes definitely won't hurt it, developing a sweeter and richer flavor.

HINTS & OPTIONS

1. Add a tablespoon of butter to the pot of sauce can add a little rich flavor. This can make it work!
2. Sprinkle some fresh grated Parmesan or your favorite grated cheese on top.
3. Yes you can use this sauce on top or pasta but to pour it over a calzone or meatball parmesan sandwich is great way to go. There's really no need usually to cook sauce for a couple of hours just for a sandwich or dipping bread into.

90 MINUTE DELICIOUS EASY TOMATO SAUCE

Prep time: 10 minutes
Cook time: 90 minutes

NOTES

You can cook this sauce for an extra 10 or 20 minutes if desired. Make sure to keep the pot covered while it's cooking and on the lowest setting possible. Make sure to stir every 20 minutes making sure the sauce on the bottom doesn't stick. Add a little water now and then to keep it from getting too thick.

Taste the sauce every 20 minutes to see how the flavor is developing. The longer you cook the sauce the richer it becomes. You can add a pinch more of salt or black pepper if you wish. This fresh sauce is easy to store in a glass jar in the refrigerator for up to 5 days or freeze for up to 3 to 4 months. Left overs sauce should be heated for 5 minutes on high heat to kill off any bacteria.

INGREDIENTS

2 (28 ounce) cans whole peeled San Marzano tomatoes or other good Italian Imported Tomatoes
1 Small Onion (finely diced)
2 TBSP Olive oil
2 Garlic Cloves (minced)
1 tsp Sugar (organic)
1 tsp Sea Salt
2 pinches (or) half of a tsp Dried Italian Herb mix
1 or 2 TBSP tomato paste
Water as needed

OPTIONS

Add 2 fresh basil leaves for extra flavor or a pinch of fresh dried red pepper flakes for extra heat.

DIRECTIONS

1. Pour the tomatoes and their juice into a large mixing bowl or crush one can at a time if the bowl isn't large enough.
2. Cut off the hard green pieces and crush the tomatoes by hand inside the bowl for a minute until the pieces are smaller.
3. Place the olive oil into a large heavy saucepan on medium heat.
4. Add garlic and simmer for 15 seconds or so.
5. Add the onion and simmer for 2 minutes or until just about translucent.
6. Pour in the all of the crushed tomatoes.
7. Next: sprinkle in the: Sugar, Salt, and all Fresh and Dried Herbs, and give a quick stir.
8. Simmer over a medium heat for 2 minutes.
9. Turn the heat down to the lowest setting.
10. Simmer for about 90 minutes.
11. Check the sauce every 20 minutes, give a quick stir with a large spoon touching the bottom of the pot, and add a little water as you see that the sauce has evaporated, mix and recover.
12. Do this every 20 minutes until the sauce reaches its peak flavor.
13. You don't have to cook the sauce the full 90 mins. Happy with the flavor? Turn off the heat.

2 QUICK PIZZA SAUCE RECIPES

Want 2 easy but great pizza sauce recipes? Well here they are. When making a Sicilian pizza I don't cook my sauce because it tastes perfect when using version # 1 below. The sauce cooks in the oven for about 24 minutes since it's a thick pizza. So there's really no need to cook the sauce first for a Sicilian pizza. This is how traditional pizza is usually made. When it comes to a regular thin crust pizza you may want to cook sauce for 5 minutes in a pan since this pizza does not make in the oven too long.

NOTES

- 1 large Sicilian pizza requires a lot of sauce, usually at least 10 ounces.
- Thin crust pizzas much less. Probably about 4 to 6 ounces, depending on the size of the pizza.
- Use either canned puree or you can make your own by taking canned Italian peeled tomatoes and puree them using a hand blender, or regular blender for a few seconds.

Version #1 NO COOK PIZZA SAUCE

INGREDIENTS

Tomato puree from Italian imported tomatoes (approx. 16 oz or less) depending on the size of pizza
Salt (2 pinches per 16 oz sauce)
Pepper (1 small pinch per16 ounces sauce)
Dried oregano powder (1 pinch per 16 oz sauce)
Optional: (1 pinch sugar)

DIRECTIONS

1. Pour sauce into a container.
2 .Add ingredients and mix well with a spoon.
3. Let it sit about for at least 30 minutes or longer so the flavors can blend.
4. Mix well before placing onto the pizza dough before baking.

Version # 2 COOK FOR 5 MINUTES PIZZA SAUCE

This is good for thin crust pizzas since they only bake for few minutes. This can help give open up the tomato flavor and give the sauce a boost in flavor.

INGREDIENTS

They're the same as in version # 1 (Just look up)

DIRECTIONS

1. In a small sauce pan over medium heat, add 1 TBSP olive oil and coat the pan or pot.
2. Add the sauce with ingredients to the pan.
3. Stir well every 30 seconds for about 5 minutes until the sauce is lightly cooked.
4. Turn off the heat and leave on stove top covered until you need it.
Either sauce can be refrigerated for 3-4 days to be used again if you don't use it all the first time.

PIZZA RECIPES
NEW YORK PIZZA

Makes: 2 Small Pizzas
Level: Advanced

INGREDIENTS

2 tsp instant dry yeast
1/3 cup lukewarm water (between 95 -100 F)
1 cup cold water
1/8 tsp salt
4 + 1/4 cups bread flour
16 oz Mozzarella cheese (use a high quality brand and thinly sliced)
12 oz tomato puree from (imported from Italy)
1/4 tsp sugar
1/8 tsp freshly ground black pepper
1/2 teaspoon dried oregano or Italian seasoning
3 Tbsp extra-virgin olive oil
4 to 7 leaves fresh basil (optional)
(Option) sprinkle a little Parmesan cheese (high quality only)

DIRECTIONS

If not using an electric stand mixer with a dough hook attachment then here are directions for making the dough by hand in a mixing bowl. If using a stand mixer you can place all of the ingredients into the bowl after you finish step #3.

1. Add sugar and yeast to a large mixing bowl of lukewarm water, mix with finger or fork for 15 seconds. The water should be about as warm as your finger or your body temp.

2. Let stand for 5-10 minutes to proof. You will see the yeast get either cloudy or foamy. You can use any type of yeast.

3. Add the cold water to the water with yeast and give a quick stir. If not using instant yeast or rapid rise yeast step #3 should only be done after step #2 and the yeast has activated in the warm water.

4. Stir in the flour gradually 1 cup at a time until all is added (mixing with a large tablespoon).

5. After the dough is firm enough, remove it from the bowl, and place on either a floured surface.

6. Sprinkle the salt evenly across the dough.

7. Knead until smooth (usually about 10 minutes) either using your hands or use the machine on low. In the machine the dough is finished when it climbs up the hook just a little.

8. Divide into two pieces (to create 2 pizzas) roll into 2 separate balls.

9. Coat the dough balls with olive oil, and place in an airtight container or a bowl with plastic wrap, in a warm spot of the house, for about 1 to 2 hours.

10. When the dough doubles in size it is ready.

11. An option, to enhance the flavor of the dough is to refrigerate it in a sealed container for 24 - 48 hours.

12. Before assembling your pizza make sure the dough is at room temperature (and out of the refrigerator or at least 1 hour).

13. After removing the dough from the container, press down a little to make it flat, and let it rest for at least 15 minutes.

14. Place a pizza stone on the lowest rack, in the oven.

15. Pre-heat oven to 550 degrees F.

16. Use only one ball of dough at a time to make 1 pizza.

17. Use a hard (lightly floured) surface to place the dough on.

18. Carefully shape the dough with your hands by pressing it down and lightly stretching it to the size and shape you'd like without tearing it.

19. If using a peel, dust it with flour before placing the dough on it.

20. You can transfer the naked pizza dough to the peel, before placing the sauce and cheese on it if you'd like.

21. Also lightly dust the dough with flour, and stretch gradually until it is the desired size that will fit on the tray or pizza stone.

22. If you are not using a pizza stone or do not have a peel to lift the pizza for transporting it to the oven you can make it on a baking tray that is greased with oil or butter.

23. Place and spread the sauce thinly over the dough, with the back of a ladle or large spoon, leaving about an inch of the edges dry without sauce.

24. Sprinkle a pinch or two of some fresh finely ground black pepper, and sprinkle oregano on top of the sauce.

25. If you'd like, as an option you can now sprinkle (very lightly) parmesan cheese for an extra kick of flavor.

26. Carefully and evenly place thinly sliced or shredded mozzarella cheese over the sauce.

27. Drizzle a small amount of olive oil over the top either before baking or after the pizza is done if you'd like some extra flavor.

28. If placing the pizza into the oven with a peel, use quick and short back and forth jerks, to ensure that the dough will slide off of the peel easily.

29. Place the far end tip of the peel touching the back of the preheated pizza stone, and remove peel with short jerks so that the pizza slides onto the stone.

30. Do not drop the pizza off the stone! If you do not think you can handle this then please use a baking tray instead.

31. Bake for approx 4 to 6 minutes in the preheated oven or until the cheese is bubbling. Try not to burn the cheese. Use the cheese as a guideline. It may take a couple more minutes if using a baking tray instead of the pizza stone.

32. Remove from the pizza from the oven by sliding the peel under the pizza, or you can use some long metal tongs to grab the pizza and pull it onto a baking tray or peel.

33. Option: place a few fresh basil leaves over the pizza as soon as it comes out of the oven.

34. Wait between 3 to 4 minutes before slicing. This will give the cheese time to firm up a bit so it will not stick and get pulled off.

35. Top with your favorite toppings for example: granulated garlic, Parmesan cheese, even red pepper flakes. Enjoy!

SICILIAN PIZZA PIE

Makes one Large Pie (12 large slices)
Level: Intermediate

TOOLS NEEDED

- A baker's half sheet aluminum pan (approximately 18"x13"x1")
- A sturdy metal spatula (to lift the pieces and serve when done)

NOTES

Try to get as close to the pan dimensions as possible. Too small or large affects the end product.

You can use a large round deep dish pan but the pan size above is recommended.

Using a round pan is okay but use a 14 or 16 inch pan. A12 inch pan will probably be too small, and require you making two pizzas which defeats the purpose of this pie.

A Sicilian pie DOESN'T require stretching the dough. You'll place the dough directly into a generously oiled pan, oiling especially the sides, and corners, for easy removal.

Sicilian pizza requires more time in the oven since it's thicker but make sure the dough is on the wetter side for a puffier crust which is what you're looking for.

The dough should rise in a bowl for between 60 to 90 minutes before placing it in the pan.

Let the dough rise inside the pan again the second time for about 20 minutes after pressing it down to fill in the pan. But don't press it down after it rises in the pan the second time.

The timing depends on the room temperature - warmer the room the faster the dough will rise.

This pie can be baked a few different ways. Either way, it's simple to make so don't freak out.

When baking anything you should check its color frequently and not only go by oven temps.

If you are not using a convection oven which bakes evenly, make sure to turn the tray halfway in the middle of the baking time. This is what the pros do in pizza shops, especially when using a hot wood burning oven for a more evenly baked pizza.

TOPPINGS

When using toppings don't use too much. This is better for pizza baking usually. For example: sprinkling a few handfuls of fresh veggies and another few handfuls of your favorite meat is fine but don't go crazy putting too much on. This will affect the baking time and may cause the pizza to burn on the bottom and be undercooked in the middle.

Toppings should be thinly sliced with some space in between them. The good news is that a Sicilian Pizza is usually more forgiving than a thin crust pie. But don't take advantage of this and overdo it.

Try not to use canned ingredients because they usually contain lots of water and usually taste weird. I always prefer to use fresh ingredients for toppings over canned.

The only ingredient from a can that I like to use is the main ingredient which is tomatoes. But they should be imported from Italy or taste like it! They shouldn't have a bitter or aluminum aftertaste.

Sicilian Pizza is traditionally served plain without toppings. Sometimes they're even made without cheese but only tomatoes or red sauce with Pecorino Romano Cheese sprinkled on top. People love pepperoni as a topping on but I prefer deli turkey meat torn into 2 inch squares.

THE DOUGH

In the past I learned the hard way use more water in the dough and keep it on the wetter side even if it's difficult to handle. This will cause it to be fluffier and more air inside when baking and this is exactly what is needed for this end result. Sicilian pizza crust is known for being light and airy.

If the dough is sticking to your hands or stand mixer too much then add some extra flour, a little at a time. Plus you can use it to clean your hands off when you're finished. Just make sure not to make the dough too dry though or your bread will be too heavy and hard inside.

The only thing you want to be crispy is the bottom and edges.

I frequently add more water or flour when making the dough. Just make small adjustments when mixing or kneading.

IMPORTANT

If making two small pies remember to divide the sauce into two portions and that this pizza is the type of pizza you press down into the pan, not stretch as you would with a thin crust pie.

3 WAYS TO BAKE THIS PIE

Since this pie can be assembled and baked various ways. Included are directions for 2 methods listed.

1. **Single Bake**. This is an easy one time bake session. See the directions below.

2. **Double Bake**. You will bake the dough twice. This is a great way to make crispy well done crust with less chance of the cheese on top getting too dark or burning, since the pie will be in the oven much longer than a thin crust pie. See directions for this method also.

3. Cheese First Single Bake. This is another simple method and although some like this I didn't. For this method you'll place the cheese right onto the dough first before adding the sauce. This causes the cheese to bake into the dough. This is simple you just reverse the steps for the sauce and cheese when assembling this pie and it's a regular single bake method.

You can have fun and play around with these various Sicilian Pizza baking methods. Just remember that this is a thick pizza and the dough should be cooked well in the center without burning the bottom or sides. Accomplish this and you'll most likely have made a super delicious pie!

INGREDIENTS (Making the Dough)

4 + 1/2 cups Flour (pizza dough flour preferred)
1/4 cup extra flour (later if needed if the dough is too moist)
3 or 4 TBSP Olive Oil
2 tsp Instant Yeast
1 TBSP Sugar
1 TBSP Salt
1 Cup Warm Water in a small bowl (lukewarm but not hot)
1/2 Cup Cold Water

INGREDIENTS (Making the Sauce) Don't cook it

16 oz Italian Crushed tomatoes (from a can or jar from Italy).
2 TBSP of Clean Water (Purified, Spring or Distilled)
1 tsp Black Pepper Powder
1 tsp Sugar
1 tsp of Salt
1 tsp Dried Basil Powder (or you can use oregano powder instead)

Option: You can also use a thick puree sauce (not paste) instead of crushed tomatoes.
Just make sure it's a high quality brand, preferably one imported from Italy.
If you can't find Imported Italian tomatoes use Hunt's brand or any decent tasting brand

INGREDIENTS (Assembling the Pizza)

12 to16 oz (about 300 grams) Mozzarella Cheese (use a great quality cheese)
6 to 8 TBSP Pecorino Romano Cheese (grated).
2 tsp dried oregano

Options: You can use a substitute for the Pecorino Cheese, something like Reggiano-Parmigiana or Grana Padano cheese imported from Italy (or a combo). Read the cheese chapter of this book

DIRECTIONS (Making the Sauce)

Note: You will NOT cook this tomato sauce. The sauce will cook on top of the pizza while baking in the oven.
1. Make sure the crushed tomatoes you're using are well crushed and not a cheap brand. If using whole tomatoes crush them by hand over a bowl or use a blender for 5 seconds.
2. Cut off and discard any hard green pieces where the stem attached to the tomato and also remove any pieces of skin with a knife.
3. If the canned tomatoes are diced and not crushed then you'll need to blend them or crush them well with a potato masher so they'll turn into more of a puree, but they are not recommended.
4. Next add all of the sauce ingredients listed above with the 2 TBSP of water in a large cup or bowl and mix well with a fork.
5. You can put this sauce into the refrigerator for 30 to 60 minutes while waiting for the dough to rise. The longer the herbs soak in the sauce the better flavor it can develop.

DIRECTIONS (Making the Dough)

1. Add yeast to the small bowl of the lukewarm water with a pinch or two of sugar and mix it well for a few seconds with a fork. Then let it sit on the counter for about 10 minutes.
2. While the yeast is finished activating add that liquid mixture with all of the water called for into the mixing bowl.
3. Next add 4 +1/2 cups flour with the salt and sugar and mix for 1 minute on low using machine, or if mixing by hand use tablespoon for about 2 minutes.
4. Add the olive oil and blend everything together using a large spoon for a few minutes and then knead for approximately 12 minutes until the dough is smooth.

5. If using an electric stand mixer, set the speed to medium for 2 minutes and then turn it down to low for another 10 minutes.

6. When the dough climbs up the hook and is smooth then it's finished.

7. Next, grease a very large container, bowl, or mixing bowl.

8. Remove the dough from the mixing bowl and place it into a large clean oiled mixing bowl.

9. Then cover it tightly with plastic wrap or aluminum foil about an hour at room temperature until the dough has risen and doubled in size. If you live in a cold climate or you're in winter season then place the dough in the warmest place you can find in the house. If not it may take a long time to rise or maybe not at all.

DIRECTIONS (Assembling the Pizza)

Important: If using the Double Bake Method do not assemble the pizza with sauce or cheese until it has baked for 10 minutes and has cooled for 30 minutes.

1. After, the dough has doubled in size then it's time to pre heat the oven to 475 degrees.

2. Punch the air out of the ball till the gas escapes. Then lift the dough or dump it out onto the well oiled baking pan.

3. Press down the dough with your palms to flatten it, until it fills about half of the pan. Do not stretch the dough. This is a Sicilian Pizza and the dough is only pressed down.

4. After 2 minutes continue to press the dough with your palms trying to even it out more while attempting to fill most of the pan.

5. Be patient because this should take about 10 minutes. Gently press the dough to fill as much of the pan as you can. The longer you do this the easier it will be for it to reach all of the sides and corners. You will most likely have a hard time for it to fill the corners properly, but that's perfectly normal. Try to gently stretch the 4 corners of the dough as explained in step # 6.

6. You will quickly and gently lift the dough corners, one corner at a time, towards the corners of the pan, up in the air about 2 inches. After you do this once you may need to do it again.

7. After about 10 minutes of fighting with the dough it will eventually give in and lose lots of its elastic bounce back action and will start to stick to its intended destinations. When you see this happen do not touch it anymore because it needs to now rest there and rise for a few more minutes.

8. In about 10 or 15 minutes you should see the dough become slightly puffy and rise. This is a good thing and is what you're looking for. DO NOT FLATTEN IT AGAIN.

9. The dough should be ready for the sauce now and you can now start to put most of the tomato sauce (about 70%) on top of the dough and spread it evenly. Try to keep it away from the edges and corners by about half of an inch or 2 cm.

10. You can now generously and evenly sprinkle the grated cheese, then place the Mozzarella cheese down next. Very lightly sprinkle some oregano powder evenly on top.

DIRECTIONS (Baking the Pizza) Single Bake Method

1. Place the pan in a pre-heated 475 degrees F oven for about 15 minutes on the center rack.

2. Take the pan out of the oven and use the remaining tomato sauce. Place it carefully with a teaspoon making about 12 large circles of sauce coving the top of the pizza.

3. Place the pan back into the oven (rotating it to cook evenly) for about 15 more minutes.

4. Check on it after more 7 minutes and look at the cheese to see if it's fully melted and bubbling. When you that 10% or less of the surface has small light brown spots then the pizza should be done baking.

5. Do not burn the cheese and don't even bake the pizza to the point where most of the cheese is developing a yellow color. The cheese won't be chewy but will be hard.

6. Remove the pan from oven and let the pizza cool for about 5 minutes before attempting to cut slices or removing the pizza from the pan.

7. To remove the pizza, first loosen the edges of the pizza from the pan with a thin knife. And try to take the pizza out of the pan with a couple of large spatulas or one spatula and a large flat plate to pick it up. You will want to loosen all four corners of the pie first with the spatula. Then try to loosen the middle of the pie with the spatula.

8. Next, pick it up using two large plates or a large tray and place it onto a large area to cut it.

9. Cut into either 9 or 12 slices whatever you prefer.

10. You're finally done, congrats. Now you can serve this great pizza and enjoy.

DIRECTIONS (Baking the Pizza Using the Double Bake Method)

You will use the same pizza assembly steps as above except you will not take the pizza out of the oven after 15 minutes to add the extra circles of sauce to it. You will do that all at the same time after you place the mozzarella cheese down and drip the extra circles of sauce on top of the cheese before baking with this method.

1. If baking the dough twice as I frequently do for a crispier crust, you'll bake the pizza dough for about 10 minutes before adding any sauce or cheese.

2. You'll then remove the pan from the oven and let it cool for about 20 to 30 minutes leaving the pizza to cool inside the pan. After the dough has cooled for about 20 or 30 minutes you can then add the sauce cheese and any topping before baking it again.

3. The second and final bake will be done ONLY for about 20 minutes (not the complete 30 minutes as required in the single bake method).

4. You should check on the color of the cheese after the pizza has been in the oven for 10 minutes during its second baking session to take precautions from burning the cheese. This is extremely important when baking things like Pizza, Bread, or Cookies.

SEE THE SINGLE BAKE METHOD DIRECTIONS FOR THE BASICS AND DIFFERENCES

NOTES & TIPS

When using the double bake method you'll add your ingredients to the dough after the dough bakes and cools. Don't mess up this part. And there's no need to reserve any sauce.

Just save about 12 teaspoons of sauce to decorate the pie with on top of the Mozzarella the last 5 minutes it's in the oven.

If there's any tomato sauce left over you can use it for making Pizza Bagels or English muffin bagels.

CHICAGO DEEP DISH PIZZA

Makes: 1 medium pizza
Level: Advanced

INGREDIENTS

2 or 3 tsp instant dry yeast
1 + 1/2 tsp white sugar (organic preferred)
1 + 1/8 cups warm water (approx 90 - 98 degrees F - warm to touch)
3 cups all-purpose flour
4 TBSP cup sunflower oil
4 TBSP cup melted butter
2 tsp sea salt or kosher salt
8 to 10 oz tomato puree or crushed peeled tomatoes (imported from Italy)
12 oz Mozzarella cheese (thinly sliced, good quality)
Italian seasoning (2 or 3 pinches)
2 tsp Parmesan cheese (good quality)

DIRECTIONS (Making the dough)

1. Add yeast and sugar warm water into a large mixing bowl and mix with fork.

2. Let it sit for 5 to 10 minutes until the yeast begins to get creamy or foamy.

3. Into the yeast water mixture add: the flour, sunflower oil, melted butter and salt and mix well for 2 minutes with a tablespoon or a stand mixer with a hook attachment.

4. If using a stand mixer, mix on low for about 10 minutes. If kneading by hand, knead for about 12 minutes or until dough is smooth.

5. Form the dough into a ball, and transfer it to a bowl which has been coated with oil or butter and wipe some of the excess butter or oil onto the dough ball with your hands.

6. Cover the bowl with plastic wrap or towel and allow dough to rise at room temperature until it doubles in size (approx 1 to 2 hours).

7. Punch down the dough to get some of the air out and let sit resting for 10 to 15 minutes.

8. While the dough is resting, preheat the oven to 425 F for at least 20 minutes, or until it's reached 425 F.

9. Press the dough into a 10 or 12 inch "deep dish" pizza pan. Let the dough press up against the sides running upward about 1 inch, then let it rest for 10 minutes before continuing.

10. Add tomato sauce with a spoon evenly except for the edges, and leave room for the crust to stay dry against the sides about 1/2 of an inch.

11. Lightly sprinkle a pinch or two or Italian seasoning, along with the Parmesan cheese.

12. Add the mozzarella cheese, and sprinkle any additional toppings you'd like to add.

13. Bake the pizza for approx 25 minutes, or until the crust is a light golden brown or the cheese bubbling with only a few speckled brown spots on top or less.

14. Remove from oven. Wait about 3 minutes, then cut slices and dig in!

Option: Have fun with pizza. Add your favorite cooked meat or veggies on top. You can even turn this into a barbeque chicken pizza if you desire. (Continue to the next page for that bonus recipe)

How to Turn this Pizza into a Barbeque Chicken Pizza

1. Have 1 chicken breast pre-cooked. Boil one quickly in about 5 minutes by following these steps.

2. Put about 2 inches of water in a pan, and heat the water on high until it boils.

3. Add a TBSP of butter to the water, then gently place the chicken breast into the boiling water.

4. Cook about 90 seconds then flip it over and cook an additional 60-90 seconds.

5. Check to see if it's cooked inside by cutting open the thickest part with a knife. If the center has changed from pink to white, it's done. But if not don't worry it will cook more in the oven.

6. Remove from heat immediately. Plate it and cut into 1/2 inch cubes.

7 Sprinkle it onto the top of the pizza and add a little extra mozzarella on top of the chicken before baking the pie for extra juiciness and flavor.

8. Instead of using the full amount of the tomato sauce in the directions, you can reduce that down to about half if you'd like, or you can skip the tomato sauce completely if you want to have a white pizza with barbeque sauce, but I always prefer having both the tomato and barbeque sauces.

9. Now add your favorite barbeque sauce (about 5 TBSP) carefully distributed on top of each piece of chicken. Get the chicken saturated to prevent it from drying out when baking the pie.

10. Bake according to the instructions above in the Chicago pizza recipe or you can even add this topping onto the Sicilian pizza recipe, either way, it will be delicious, and the baking time should be about the same.

Just please make sure the chicken breast is very fresh and not sitting in the freezer for many months. If it's not fresh it will give the pizza a real weird old chicken flavor.

Notes

Don't overload the pizza with 3 pounds of ingredients, less is always better. Too many ingredients can make it soggy, watery and undercooked.

When placing the veggies or meat on the pizza leave space between the pieces for air to circulate. An example: 2 handfuls of meat and a 2 handfuls of veggies sprinkled around evenly, is the ideal amount for a 10-14 inch pizza.

Pizza Dough Tips

Be sure to use a large enough container about twice the size of the dough to allow the dough to rise. If refrigerating the dough overnight remove it at least one hour before using it to help it warm up.

Pizza Sauce Tips

The amount of sauce and cheese you place on the dough depends on the size of the pizza. Try using common sense when following recipe instructions and adjust accordingly. Don't put too much sauce on most pizza but this one can handle more than the other thinner types.

Transporting Pizzas

If ever using a pizza stone when making a thin crust pizza or calzone be careful not to drop the pizza on the floor when placing or removing it from the oven. For beginners it may best to make your first pizza directly on a baking tray. I'm speaking of a New York Pizza or a Neapolitan Pizza.

These are usually made not using pizza trays that require them to have a tall border as the Sicilian or Deep Dish does. Plus you may prefer making the pizza a few times before going out and investing in a pizza baking stone and a peel. However stones are good for baking other things like calzones, beads and other stuff, not just pizza. Pizza making is fun and when you get the hang of it you may want to advance your skills by letting the dough sit overnight or 2 days in the fridge to develop more flavor.

NEW YORK CALZONE

Makes 2 medium or 4 small Calzones
Level: Easy

INGREDIENTS

4 + 1/4 cups bread flour
1 +1/4 tsp instant dry yeast or fast rise yeast
1/3 cup (approx) lukewarm water to touch
1 cup cold water
1/8 tsp salt
18 to 20 oz whole milk mozzarella cheese sliced or shredded (a high quality brand preferred)
6 to 8 oz Ricotta Cheese (choose a delicious brand)
1/4 tsp sugar

DIRECTIONS

1. In a large mixing bowl, add the yeast and sugar with 1/3 cup of lukewarm water.

2. Mix with you finger or fork for 20 seconds. The water should be just a little warmer than your body temp.

3. Now let that sit for 10 minutes to proof. You will see it get either: creamy, cloudy, a little bubbly, or foamy.

4. Add the 1 cup of cold water to the yeast water and give a quick stir.

5. Add the flour and stir it in gradually for a few minutes (about 1 cup at a time) until it's all incorporated, using a large spoon, or a stand mixer with a dough hook attachment.

6. When the dough becomes firm, move it from the bowl to either a floured surface continue using your stand mixer.

7. Sprinkle the salt evenly across the dough.

8. Knead the dough until smooth (usually about 12 minutes by hand or 10 minutes if using the machine) set to low. A stand mixer or bread machine is preferred. When the dough climbs up the hook it's done.

9. Divide into 2 or 4 equal portions, enough to make either 2 large or 4 medium calzones. Then roll portions into separate balls.

10. Lightly coat the dough balls by rubbing a little bit of olive oil on them with your hands.

11. Place the balls in a large container or separate containers covered with plastic wrap. Do not let them touch each other.

12. Keep them at room temperature, in a non-drafty part of the house or kitchen for about 90 minutes until they double in size. Then they are ready to form your calzone.

13. You can even refrigerate the dough it in a sealed container for either 1 or 2 days before you'd like to make the calzone. Just remember to make sure each container is much larger for the dough to rise.

14. Before you create your calzone, make sure the dough is at room temperature and has been out of the refrigerator for at least an hour.

15. Pre-heat the oven to 525 degrees F. It must be hot before baking.

16. Remove the dough from the container and press it down a little to make it flat. This gives it a chance to rest. Wait for at least 5 minutes and let it sit there.

17. When using pizza stone "it must" be heated in the oven when the oven is pre-heated. Do not put the cold pizza stone into a hot oven. They must be the same temp or won't turn out good but a cold baking tray can be added to the oven when baking.

18. Use only one ball for each calzone you want to make. Keep them separated from each other while baking.

19. Use a hard (lightly floured) surface to place the dough on.

20. Shape the dough by pressing it down with your palms stretching it out only a little. You do not want this too thin or it will tear and the cheese will come out.

21. Divide both cheeses into portions for the same number of calzones you'll be making.

22. When shaping the dough it's similar to the shape of a pizza. You will make a regular circle shape as you would for a pizza.

23. Next, put mozzarella cheese on one side only. Do NOT put the cheese too close to the sides.

24. Then gently place a couple heaping Tablespoons of the Ricotta cheese on top of the mozzarella cheese.

25. Sprinkle a couple of pinches of Parmesan cheese onto of the Ricotta cheese, along with a pinch of salt. The parmesan cheese may be salty enough for you though.

26. You are now going to fold the other half of the dough over the top to make a half circle. Do this in one fast motion using two hands.

27. Press the dough with your fingers to seal all of the edges where it meets the other side, so none of the cheese can escape.

28. With a sharp knife make 2 or 3 small slits on top center to the dough to let steam escape while baking.

29. You assemble this right inside the baking tray if using one and this is the easiest way to bake a calzone because it's heavy and difficult to transport. I suggest doing it this way unless you're experienced because you cannot rip the dough, or the cheese will come out while baking.

30. If using a pizza stone you will need a well-floured peel to slide the calzone into the oven. This is tricky because the calzone will be heavy as I mentioned and you don't want it sticking or dropping. So either use a very flat well-floured tool to transport it or bake it on a tray.

31. Bake for about 15-20 minutes depending on your individual oven and varying temperature.

32. You will see the dough get dry on top and the sides getting darker which is a pretty good indicator that the calzone is ready. Check the bottom with a spatula and do not let it burn.

33. Remove and let cool for 3 minutes before serving.

34. Serve with your favorite tomato sauce for dipping and enjoy.

CALZONE NOTES

When mixing and kneading dough for calzone, pizza or bread a stand mixer machine is always recommended for convenience sake. Most chefs use a heavy duty stand mixer with a dough hook attachment or they wouldn't be able to keep up with the work they do.

They're great for making: bread, pizza, calzone, desserts, crèmes and fillings and usually come with a few different attachments for the specific recipes you're making. When baking the calzone, make sure to check it after 10 or 12 minutes to see how it's baking. Get a spatula and lift up the bottom to make sure it's starting to turn a light golden color, but that it's not burning.

The inside containing the cheese takes a long time to cook so just be careful not to burn the outside or bottom. It's better for the inside to be a little cold then to burn the outside. Just turn off the oven and let it sit in the hot oven to continue baking the cheese inside.

Sometimes the top and sides of the Calzone don't always change color when it's finished baking, but the bottom will be your main indicator. Test the dough on top with a sharp knife to see how it's coming along. Check out the kitchen tools page on my website at mariomazzo.com/kitchen-tools for great stuff.

MAIN COURSES & PASTA DISHES
CHICKEN PARMESAN

Serves: 4
Level: Intermediate
Needed: 1 or 2 large frying pans

INGREDIENTS (for Chicken)

4 boneless, skinless chicken breasts fresh or defrosted, pounded thin
Salt and freshly ground black pepper
2 cups all-purpose flour, seasoned with salt and a pinch of pepper
4 large eggs, beaten with 2 tablespoons water and seasoned with salt
2 cups of good quality bread crumbs (Panko preferred)
1 cup pure olive oil, sunflower or safflower oil (no canola or soy oil)
1 pound fresh mozzarella, thinly sliced
1/4 cup freshly grated Parmesan (Parmigiano-Reggiano preferred) substitutions can be: Grana Padano, or Pecorino Romano cheese
Fresh basil leaves or parsley (for a garnish)

INGREDIENTS (for Quick Tomato Sauce)

2 tablespoons olive oil
3 cloves garlic, crushed
A few pinches of little sea salt or kosher salt to make a garlic paste
2 (28-oz) cans plum tomatoes and their juices, pureed in a blender
1 (16-oz) can crushed tomatoes
1 small can of tomato paste (approx 6 oz)
1 bay leaf
Salt and pepper
Optional -1 small bunch of Italian parsley
Optional -2 pinches of dry basil

DIRECTIONS: (for Quick 50 Minute Tomato Sauce)

1. Heat a tablespoon of olive oil over medium heat in a large saucepan.

2. Add garlic and onions and cook until the onions are translucent (about 2-3 minutes).

3. Add the can of pureed tomatoes and also add the can of crushed tomatoes and mix.

4. Next add the can of tomato paste by scooping it out the paste. Keep the can and then add approx 4 ounces of water to the empty can and empty the remains into saucepan.

5. Add the bay leaf, a pinch of basil, with 4 or 5 pinches of salt and stir well.

6. Optional, add a few pinches of fresh parsley.

7. Bring to a light boil.

8. Reduce heat to the "lowest" setting and cover saucepan with top.

9. Cook for about 30 minutes then check to see is the sauce is well blended with all ingredients. Then stir from the bottom for about 30 seconds.

10. Add about 3 ounces of water if the sauce is getting too thick or dry. Cover the pot and cook on lowest setting approx for an additional 20 minutes.

11. Optional - season with salt and pepper to taste.

DIRECTIONS: (Making the Chicken)

1. Preheat oven to 425 degrees F for at least 10 -15 minutes.

2. Season the chicken lightly on both sides with salt.

3. Dredge (coat) each breast separately in the flour and tap to get rid of off excess

4. Dip in the egg and then wait a couple seconds for any excess to drip off.

5. Dredge on both sides in the bread crumbs.

6. Divide oil between 2 large stainless steel frying pans if you have two pans. If using one pan save about half the oil for making your second batch.

7. Heat oil over high heat before adding chicken, but DO NOT let the oil smoke.

8. Add 2 chicken breasts to each pan and cook until golden brown on both sides (approx) 2 minutes on each side.

9. Transfer chicken to lasagna tray or baking sheet.

10. Top each breast with as much tomato sauce as you desire, then a spoon of grated parmesan cheese, and a few slices of mozzarella cheese with salt and pepper to taste.

11. Bake in the oven until the chicken is cooked well and the cheese is melted (approx 5 -10 minutes). If you do not pound the chicken breasts thing then you can cook a little longer.

12. Remove from the oven and let sit for 1 minute before serving.

13. Optional: Garnish with parsley leaves or any garnish you like.

If you would like to make a Chicken Parmesan Sub Sandwich just follow that recipe in this book!

Other Important Stuff

Option: If you want your chicken to be a little juicier, don't pound it too thin. You'll have to let it cook a little longer since it's thicker. If using factory made sauce it probably won't taste as good, but if do try to use one that you already know tastes great. If using pre-made sauce use approx 2 (32 oz jars) containers of sauce or a little less. Make sure to buy the best tasting sauce possible if you must use a pre-made sauce. Use a stainless steel pan for this recipe and the rest in this book.

See the chapter called Types of Pots & Pans to Use, so you can see why to use a stainless steel pan.

EGGPLANT PARMESAN

Serves: 6
Level: Intermediate

INGREDIENTS (for the Sauce)

3 TBSP extra-virgin olive oil
5 cloves garlic (pressed or grated)
2 or 3 medium yellow onions, peeled, halved and cut into thin slices
Sea salt or kosher salt
1 tsp granulated sugar
2 pinches off finely ground black or white pepper
(3) 28-oz cans San Marzano whole pealed or crushed-peeled tomatoes
(Option) 1 tablespoon red pepper flakes (for little additional spice and heat)

INGREDIENTS (for the Eggplant)

3 medium eggplants (approx 2-3 pounds total) washed + cut into 1/4 to1/2-inch-thick slices
Sea Salt or Kosher salt
1 cup all-purpose flour
5 large eggs
3 TBSP whole milk
5 cups Italian-style breadcrumbs
1 TBSP dried oregano
1 TBSP fresh thyme leaves
Vegetable oil, for frying, as needed (1+1/2 to 2 cups)
1 + 1/2 pounds mozzarella (cut into thin slices)
1/2 cup grated parmesan cheese
1/2 cup grated provolone

DIRECTIONS (Making the Sauce)

1. Pour the tomatoes into a large mixing bowl and crush them by hand.

2. In a sauce pan heat the olive oil.

3. Add the garlic and onions and cook until the onions are translucent (about 3 minutes) on low heat.

4. Add a few pinches of salt, a pinch or two of black pepper and 1 tsp of sugar. Stir well and then add the optional red pepper flakes.

5. Add the tomatoes and use a wooden spoon or potato masher to break up some of the larger tomato pieces.

6. Cover the pan and cook over low heat for about 20 minutes.

7. Stir then taste to see if the tomatoes need a little more salt and add according to taste.

8. The tomatoes should be fairly broken down and the flavors starting to come together a little.

9. Cook for 10 more minutes and then taste it again to see if the sauce is thickening. If sauce is getting too thick you can always add 2 ounces of water at a time. Mix well and cook 5 more minutes, then turn off the heat.

DIRECTIONS (Making the Eggplant)

1. Salt each slice of eggplant on both sides.

2. Place the eggplant slices on either 2 baking sheets, a few large plates, or in a collider with a bowl underneath so you can see how much water is released.

3. Allow it to sit for about 45 minutes or, until you see the salt drawing lots of the liquid and the bitter flavor out. Dump all the bitter water into the sink.

4. Rinse with cold water and dry them with a paper towel or clean kitchen towel. Make sure no pieces of towel get attached to the eggplant.

5. Preheat the oven to 425 degrees F.

6. Put the flour in a medium bowl.

7. In a second bowl, whisk together the eggs and milk.

8. Using, a third bowl, combine the breadcrumbs with the oregano and fresh thyme leaves.

9. Dip each eggplant slice into the flour and shake off any excess flour.

10. Dip each eggplant slice into the egg mixture.

11. Dip (press firmly) each eggplant slice into the breadcrumbs. Coat both sides of each slice.

12. Arrange the slices in single layers onto the two baking sheets or plates.

13. In a large skillet, pour approximately 1 cup or less of oil to fill the pan about 1/2-inch.

14. Heat the oil until just "before" smoking lightly, or you can test with a thermometer and wait until it registers between 380 and 400 degrees F.

15. Use a pair of kitchen tongs or large long fork to add a single layer of the eggplant to the oil.

16. Cook for about 2 minutes on each side or until golden brown.

17. Remove from the oil and transfer to a baking sheet fitted with 3 layers of paper towels for absorbing the grease, while the next batch is cooking.

18. Season each batch with a few pinches of salt.

19. Add a little more fresh oil into the pan with the old oil bringing it back to the same heat level.

20. Add another batch to the skillet, and repeat until all the eggplant is cooked.

DIRECTIONS (Assembling the Eggplant)

1. In a 12 x 17 inch baking dish or two smaller baking dishes, spoon in some of the tomato sauce until it generously coats the bottom of baking dish.
2. Place one layer of the fried eggplant into the baking dish.
3. The eggplant slices can overlap some. It doesn't need to be perfect.
4. Top with a thin layer of the mozzarella sliced cheese.
5. Sprinkle with about one fourth of the parmesan and provolone cheeses.
6. Spoon more sauce on top and repeat two more times to make 3 layers.
7. On the very top layer use the remaining mozzarella.
8. Place the dish into the top level of a 375 F degree oven and bake until the cheese is melted and bubbly (about 25 to 30 minutes).
9. Remove from oven and let sit for 5 to 10 minutes for the liquids to settle.
10. Top with a fresh sprinkle of parmesan cheese.
11. Cut into squares with a sharp knife and pick up with a large serving spoon or a solid spatula.
12. Enjoy!

10 MINUTE FRESH HOMEMADE PASTA

Level Easy
Ready In: 10 minutes
Serves: 2

NOTES

When making fresh pasta you can use a simple guide of 100 grams (about 3 and a one half ounce) flour to one egg. One cup of properly measured flour weighs about 120 grams. So you will add about 80% of a cup of flour to the bowl for each person you are feeding.

Always spoon the flour into the measuring cup. Never dip the cup into the flour bag or you'll pack in too much flour. You can use a pasta hand machine to stretch the dough or a rolling pin to make the pasta. If you don't have a rolling pin, use a clean wine bottle or similar long bottle.

If you can't find the exact flour below then use whatever you have on hand. If the pasta sticks to the machine you can coat it lightly with some flour. When done cutting the pasta, either cook it immediately of cover the stands by placing them in between a damp towel to keep them moist for up to a few hours. It's not really necessary to use your food processor unless you like cleaning things.

INGREDIENTS

150 grams 00 flour
50 grams semolina flour
2 large eggs (organic preferred)
1/2 teaspoon olive oil
A pinch of sea salt
Some extra flour to dusting the surface

DIRECTIONS

1. Place flour onto a large plate or into a bowl and make a hole in the middle.

2. Crack an egg into the center flour and add pinch of salt and a teaspoon of olive oil.

3. Mix with spoon for a minute or two until the dough starts to form into a ball.

4. Then switch to using your clean hands.

5. Knead the dough until smooth (about 5 minutes).

6. After the dough ball is made wrap it up tightly in plastic wrap to keep it from drying and let it rest for about 15 minutes.

7. Next, stretch out the dough using a pasta machine a few times, setting the knob for thinner pasta each time, until you reach your desired thickness. You will probably have to cut the dough in half because it will become too long. Remember that if you don't use a pasta machine you can just roll it out on a counter instead and make it the old fashioned way.

8. Cut into the desired type of pasta you'd like to eat either with the machine or cut it yourself with a knife right on the counter. Make sure to lightly coat the dough on both sides with flour before cutting.

9. Sprinkle a little flour on the pasta before cooking to help prevent sticking.

10. Separate the strands of dough and cook the pasta in salted boiling water for 1 or two minutes, while gently stirring it to avoid sticking.

11. Taste the pasta to see if it's done. Congrats, you just made your own homemade pasta just like a fancy Italian restaurant.

FETTUCCINE ALFREDO

Serves: 4
Level: Easy

INGREDIENTS

16 oz dried fettuccine (for fresh pasta add a little more)
1 + 1/2 cups of grated Parmesan Cheese (use "Parmigiano-Reggiano" for the best flavor)
8 TBSP (or 1 stick) unsalted butter. (If you like salt you can use salted butter)
2 cups heavy cream
1 TBSP olive oil
1 large or 2 small garlic cloves (finely minced)
Nutmeg (freshly grated, just 1 pinch)
(Option) Add fresh squeezed lemon juice – just a couple drops on your plate after it's served.
(Option) A pinch of finely ground white pepper to the sauce pan before adding pasta
(Option) Add cooked or grilled chicken slices on top to make this a "Chicken Fettuccini Alfredo" dish
(Option) 1 or 2 TBSP of good white wine to the sauce when it's cooking.
(Option) a small handful of fresh parsley

NOTES

You can keep the sauce separated from the pasta until ready to serve it. This is helpful for many reasons. To do this just keep the sauce in the pot until ready to eat and then you can just take a few spoons of sauce and pour it over the pasta.

If serving the pasta this way it's probably best to rinse this pasta well and then let all of the water drip off by tossing it around in a colander.

This is a good way to keep the pasta from getting too soft and sticky. Then when you're ready to eat you can place a little of the hot Alfredo sauce from the pot on top of the pasta instead of adding the pasta to the pan.

If you are ready to eat and just want to save some time: just drain all of the water off the pasta, but don't rinse it. Then toss it directly into the sauce pan or pot and heat it for 30 seconds. But this is okay when you are ready to eat.

Do not let the pasta sit in the pot too long in the water after its done cooking or it will get overcooked and mushy before adding it to the sauce pan.

LEMON JUICE

If you decide to add the optional fresh lemon juice, don't add too much. You shouldn't really taste it that much but it can give a bright clean taste.

Some add it to the sauce while cooking, but it's safer to just mix it on your plate just in case you don't like it that much. Better to play it safe.

Only use fresh squeezed juice, not the type in the little plastic bottle for this dish if deciding to try some.

DIRECTIONS

1. Start to cook the pasta in a large pot of boiling (well-salted) water stirring frequently to keep from sticking.

2. While the pasta is cooking make your Alfredo sauce. It only takes 5 minutes to make.

3. Heat a separate large skillet to low heat and add the olive oil.

4. Place minced garlic into the center of the oil and cook (for approx 30 seconds).

5. (Option) You can now add the optional splash of white wine to the garlic oil and cook off the alcohol (for approx 15 seconds).

6. Keep the heat on low so you do not burn the garlic.

7. Add the butter to the oil and stir until well until all butter is melted. Do not let it cook or bubble, just melt it.

8. Option: You can now add the pinch of freshly ground nutmeg if you have any, before adding the cream.

9. Start to pour the cream into the pan slowly while mixing for about 1 minute until all is mixed well with the butter. You can turn up the heat now to medium.

10. Continue to heat the sauce for about 2 minutes, stirring constantly, while scraping the sides of the pan, without it bubbling or boiling.

11. Add the Reggiano Parmesan cheese to the cream stirring constantly until all the cheese is blended and the sauce is creamy (for approx 2 minutes).

12. Remove the pan of cream sauce from the heat immediately.

13. Taste the Alfredo Sauce and season with salt to taste, if needed.

14. Taste the pasta to see if it's finished cooking.

15. Remove the pasta from heat.

16. Drain the water from pasta for a non-rinse, or you can rinse with water if you'd prefer and get rid of excess water by draining then shaking.

17. Add the drained pasta into the cream sauce pan or spoon the sauce over your pasta (whichever you prefer).

18. Mix well

19. Serve in a large pasta bowl or shallow individual bowls.

20. (Option) Top with fresh Parmesan cheese.

21. (Option) sprinkle fresh parsley over the pasta.

22. (Option) place some grilled chicken breast strips on top of the pasta for a Chicken Alfredo meal.

22. Buon Appetito!

BONUS (Super-Eat-Tip)

As you may already know that the sauce is always the star to me. That means any color, red, white or other. When you make the sauce 90% of the meal is done. I love pouring this sauce over garlic bread as seen on the back cover of this book.

Take a loaf or two of fresh Italian bread and make some garlic bread using the recipe in this book.

You can even grill some chicken, slice it up into thin strips and then top the garlic bread or pasta with it. What the heck, you can even melt some Mozzarella and Parmesan cheese on top of that chicken, and make a hot Chicken Alfredo Sub Sandwich! Whatever you do don't use a microwave oven.

LASAGNA with MEAT SAUCE

Serves: 6
Level: Intermediate
Needed: 9 inch x 13 inch baking dish

INGREDIENTS

1 + 3/4 pounds of very lean ground beef, (feel with fingers to remove hard little pieces)
OPTION: you can use fresh ground turkey meat instead of beef.
3/4 cup onion (finely chopped or minced)
2 large garlic cloves (crushed)
2 TBSP white sugar (organic)
1/2 tsp dried basil leaves
1/8 teaspoon fennel seed powder (chop, crush, or and grind the seeds to a powder)
1 can pealed crushed tomatoes (28 oz)
2 cans tomato paste (approx 6 oz each)
2 cans tomato sauce (approx 6 oz each)
1/2 cup water
1 tsp Italian seasoning – (or you can use a combo of any of the following -1 pinch of each: oregano, marjoram, thyme, rosemary and sage)
1/4 tsp ground black pepper
3 TBSP chopped fresh parsley
12 lasagna noodles (long thin type)
15 oz. ricotta cheese
16 oz. mozzarella cheese sliced thinly (whole milk is always preferred)
1 egg (large or extra-large size)
1 TBSP sea salt
1 TBSP cooking oil (either: sunflower, safflower or olive oil)
3/4 cup grated parmesan cheese (imported from Italy)

DIRECTIONS (Sauce & Noodles)

1. Heat a large stainless steel frying pan to medium and add the ground beef.
2. Flatten it as best you can to resemble a large pancake)
3. Cook for approximately 3 minutes and then divide it into about 6 pieces and flip them over to cook for an additional 3 minutes or until all the meat is browned on both sides.
4. Drain as much water and fat as you can from the pan using a large spoon and discard the 98% of the liquid. It doesn't have to be perfect.
5. Sprinkle the Italian seasoning and fennel on top of the meat inside the pan.
6. Break up the meat with a large spoon into little pieces.
7. Continue cooking the meat while mixing frequently (about 4 more mins), then turn off the heat.
8. Heat a "separate" large sauce pot on low heat and add 2 TBSP of cooking oil with the garlic then bring to a light sizzle for about 30 seconds.
9. Next add the chopped onion to pot and turn up the heat to medium. Stir frequently and cook until the onion is translucent for about 2 to 3 minutes.
10. Now you will transfer all of the meat from the other pan into the sauce pot but make sure you drain all of the liquid before doing so.
11. Turn down the temperature to low and stir frequently while cooking the meat for an additional minute to a light sizzle, so the meat soaks up that delicious onion and garlic flavor.

12. Stir in crushed tomatoes and give a quick stir.

13. Add tomato paste, tomato sauce, and water and give about 10 good stirs to break up the tomato paste.

14. Add the sugar, pepper, 1 TBSP of sea salt, 2 tablespoons parsley and give a quick stir.

15. Now is the time, you can add the optional (but not necessary) secret ingredient as described in my free cookbook called "Secret Ingredients" which you can download for free from my website.

16. Keep the heat to lowest setting and simmer covered (for approx 1 hour + 30 minutes) but make sure to stir every 20 minutes or so, focusing on the bottom to keep it from sticking.

17. After the sauce has cooked for about 1 hour and 20 minutes, bring a separate large pot of salted water to a boil.

18. Cook lasagna noodles for about 8 to10 minutes (or whatever the instructions read on the box).

19. Drain the noodles and rinse them with cold water to end the cooking process. Try not to break them while removing them from the pot, so do not use sharp objects.

20. In a mixing bowl, combine ricotta cheese with egg, with the remaining 1 TBSP of chopped parsley, and 1/2 teaspoon salt. Mix vigorously with a spoon until everything is combined,

21. Preheat the oven to 375 degrees F (190 degrees C). And go to the next section of directions for assembling the lasagna.

DIRECTIONS (Assembling the Lasagna)

1. First before starting: you "must" Coat the bottom of a 9 x 13 inch Baking Dish with a thin layer of sauce you just cooked (approx 1 + 1/2 cups).

2. Layer #1 = Noodles: Arranging the noodles covering the whole bottom of the pan. (You can cut the noodles to make them fit perfectly if you like).

3. Layer #2 = Ricotta Cheese: Coating the noodles by spreading them with one half of the ricotta cheese mixture with the back of a spoon.

4. Layer #3 = Mozzarella Cheese: Top the noodles with one third of mozzarella cheese slices.

5. Layer #4 = Tomato Sauce: Using a tablespoon, equally distribute about 1 + 1/2 cups of the tomato sauce over mozzarella.

6. Layer #5 = Parmesan Cheese: Sprinkle the sauce with 1/4 cup of the Parmesan cheese.

7. Now repeat the exact same steps of Layers #1 through #5 again – You'll be doing this twice. Then see the next step and make the final three touches.

8. The final three touches will be to add the remaining sauce, then the remaining Parmesan cheese, and finally the remaining mozzarella cheese as the last ingredient on the very top.

9. Go to the next section now containing the baking directions.

DIRECTIONS (Baking the Lasagna)

1. Cover the baking dish with foil aluminum foil, but "make sure the foil does not touch" the cheese. You can try to prevent the cheese from sticking to the foil by greasing the inside of the foil lightly with some oil or spraying it with a light coat of cooking spray.

2. Bake in your 375 F degree preheated oven for about 20 minutes.

3. Remove foil, and bake an additional 20 mins or until all of the cheese is melted and the top and sides are lightly bubbling. Check it every 7 minutes to make sure the cheese is not burning on top.

4. Cool for approx 15 minutes to ensure all the liquid has become firm and everything is settled or it will be too soupy to serve. This is an important step.

5. After about 15 minutes, cut into small squares with a sharp serrated knife and remove the pieces with a strong spatula.

6. Serve and enjoy!

Delicious Tip

Dip your favorite fresh bread into the lasagna and enjoy. Fresh made garlic bread is definitely a recommended favorite for this dish. Check out my garlic bread recipe called Mazzo's Garlic Bread.

MAZZO'S GARLIC BREAD

Serves: 4
Level: Super Easy
Things needed: Oven Broiler or Toaster Oven, a baking sheet

INGREDIENTS

A long large loaf of Italian or French bread
4 TBSP extra virgin olive oil
4 garlic cloves
6 to 8 TBSP (or 1 stick) salted butter
Optional: fresh Grated Parmesan cheese
Optional: fresh shredded Mozzarella cheese
Optional garlic powder

Directions Using Fresh Garlic

Before starting -Take approx 1 stick (6 to 8 TBSP) salted butter out of the fridge to soften at room temp, for about 40 minutes. Never use a microwave

1. Turn on your oven broiler to low (top element only), or use a toaster oven with the top element only. You don't want to overcook this bread or make the bottom too hard.
2. Cut a fresh loaf of Italian or French bread in half the long way, inside facing up to fit into oven.
3. Lay separated pieces into the baking tray or strong aluminum foil needed to catch any melted butter.
4. Next mince 4 garlic cloves and place them into a low heated pan containing 4 tablespoons olive oil for about 15 seconds bringing it to a light sizzle and remove the pan from the heat.
5. Take the oil along with garlic pieces, spread it evenly over the top side of the bread only with a spoon.
6. Next take the softened butter on the back of a spoon or a butter knife and spread it evenly next.
7. Put only a pinch of sea salt over the top of the buttered and oiled bread..
8. Place tray or foil holding the bread into oven or toaster for about 1 to 3 minutes until edges are crisp.
9. The center should still be a little soft and chewy. You can always toast it longer later after tasting it.

Option: You can substitute the fresh minced garlic for some fresh granulated garlic powder.

But if using powder - Do not heat the garlic powder in the oil. It can burn.

Directions for Using Granulated Garlic or Powder
1. Brush olive oil onto the bread
2. Then spread the butter evenly on top of the oil or you can use both together as a mixture.
3. Finally sprinkle very lightly some granulated garlic or powder and some sea salt on the top of the bread before placing it into the oven. Granulated garlic is preferred. Garlic powder is not a bad alternative but is normally used on the table in a shaker to flavor your food. Congratulations, you've made a crazy delicious garlic bread.

SUPER GARLIC BREAD TIP

If you want to get a little crazy with your garlic bread, sprinkle a little freshly grated parmesan cheese or mozzarella cheese on top. I usually like mine plain, but when the mood hits I do this. You can deck this bread out with cheese, especially if you love cheese. If there are any cheese heads reading this, make one of each and see which you like better. Just melt the cheese for about 1 minute as a final step.

BAKED ZITI with RICOTTA

Serves 4
Level: Easy

NOTES

Use whichever type of sauce you like. I prefer to make my own. Here's a great quick recipe below for some fast tomato sauce. You do not need to cook this one too long because it cooks twice.

INGREDIENTS (for Tomato Sauce)

1 can Italian peeled tomatoes (approximately 15 ounces) crushed with your hands
1 jar or can of tomato puree (approximately of 24 ounces) not paste
1 tsp sea salt
1 pinch of black pepper powder
1 TBSP olive oil
1/4 onion (finely minced)

INGREDIENTS (for the Ziti)

15 oz Ricotta Cheese (whole milk type) you can use small curd cottage instead as a substitute
2 eggs (beaten)
1/4 cup grated parmesan cheese (use Parmigiano Reggiano)
1/4 tsp black pepper (ground powder)
2 TBSP fresh parsley (minced)
16 oz of Ziti Noodles Cooked and Drained and lightly rinsed (You can also use Rigatoni or Penne Pasta Ziti Noodles are preferred)
39 oz of your favorite tomato sauce (Use the tomato sauce recipe below or another from this book)
2 cups mozzarella cheese (shredded or chopped into small pieces)

DIRECTIONS (Making the Tomato Sauce)

1. Heat 1 TBSP of olive oil in a sauce pot over medium heat.

2. Add the minced onion and cook until translucent.

3. Add the crushed tomatoes to the pot and stir for a minute or two, heating them.

4. Add the salt and pepper.

5. Now add the tomato puree and stir well. Not paste. Paste is the consistency of toothpaste and very thick. Puree is much thinner like a tomato soup.

6. Cover the pot and cook for about 25 or 30 minutes until it tastes lightly cooked.

7. Turn off the heat and leave the pot covered.

DIRECTIONS (Making the Baked Ziti)

1. Preheat oven to 350 degrees F.

2. Drain any excess water from the ricotta cheese before adding it to the bowl using either a strainer or coffee filter.

3. In a large bowl, combine ricotta cheese, eggs, parmesan cheese and seasonings and mix well with a large spoon.

4. In another bowl, thoroughly combine cooked pasta and only about half of the cooked tomato sauce.

5. Place about one third of the half of the tomato/pasta mixture in a 9" x 12" baking dish or similar dish.

6. The next layer will be the egg and cheese mixture. Spread the entire amount on top of the pasta evenly.

7. Sprinkle 1 cup of the mozzarella cheese on top of the cheese layer.

8. Next, add 1/3 of remaining tomato/pasta mixture as the next layer.

9. Sprinkle with half of the remaining mozzarella cheese on top.

10. Bake 25 minutes. Remove the dish from oven and then sprinkle the last bit of mozzarella cheese on top. Place the dish back into the oven for about 10 to 15 minutes until the cheese is melted. The total cook time should be approximately 35-40 minutes until bubbly. Let it sit about 5 minutes before serving.

11. Serve with your favorite bread and enjoy!

NOTES

Make sure to leave about 1/3 of the tomato sauce in the pot and save it as a topping to be used at the table when ready to serve on top of the pasta and also have some extra sauce to dip bread into.

SPAGHETTI & MEATBALLS with TOMATO SAUCE

Serves: 4
Level: Easy

INGREDIENTS (FOR SAUCE)

3/4 cup onion (chopped)
5 cloves garlic (minced)
1/4 cup olive oil
2 (28 oz) cans whole peeled tomatoes
2 tsp salt
1 tsp white sugar (organic)
1 bay leaf (whole)
1 (6 oz) can of tomato paste
3/4 tsp dried basil
1/8 tsp black pepper (ground powder)

INGREDIENTS (FOR MEATBALLS)

1 lb ground beef (lean)
1 cup fresh bread crumbs
1 Tbsp dried parsley
1 Tbsp grated Parmesan Cheese
1/8 tsp ground black pepper
1/8 tsp garlic powder
1 egg beaten

INGREDIENTS (FOR SPAGHETTI)

Cook either dried or fresh spaghetti according to directions. Or you can even make your own fresh homemade pasta with the recipe in this book.

DIRECTIONS (MAKING THE MEATBALLS)

1. In a large bowl, combine the ground beef, bread crumbs, parsley, Parmesan cheese, black pepper, garlic powder and beaten egg.

2. Mix well with hands.

3. Form the mixture into 10-12 balls.

4. Wash hands.

5. Place and store the meatballs covered in the refrigerator until needed.

6. Heat a large saucepan over low-medium heat.

7. Put in the olive oil, garlic, and onion.

8. Sauté until the onion is translucent or soft (approx. 2-3 minutes).

9. Stir in tomatoes, salt, sugar and bay leaf.

10. Cover, reduce heat to low, and simmer 90 minutes.

11. When the 90 minutes is almost complete (about 85 minutes), heat up a second pan to cook the raw meatballs in. (preferably a large omelet pan).

12. Cook only about 5-7 minutes or so, turning every minute with a spoon, until all sides are very lightly browned and they start to release the fat and grease.

13. Immediately turn of the heat of the pan holding the meatballs.

14. After the tomatoes have been cooking for 90 minutes stir the tomato paste, basil, pepper into the tomatoes to make your sauce.

15. Stir the tomato sauce for a minute to get the paste mixed well.

16. At this point you will take the meatballs one by one with a spoon and add them into the sauce.

17. Simmer with everything together in one pan for an additional 30-45 minutes, or until all of the flavors are blended.

18. Taste and serve.

DIRECTIONS (MAKING THE SPAGHETTI)

It's simple to serve the meatballs with spaghetti.

1. Boil some water in a separate pot while the meatballs are almost finished cooking.

2. Either: follow the instructions on the package, or make your own fresh pasta with the easy homemade pasta recipe in this book.

3. The cooking time is usually around 4 minutes for angel hair and up to about 9 minutes for thicker regular spaghetti.

4. Taste the pasta when it's almost done by pulling a single stand out of the pot with a fork while it's still boiling and bite into it to see if it's cooked in the center.

5. Rinse and drain in a colander or you can use the no rinse method in this cookbook.

SERIOUS EATER TIP

Want to have some fun and like to eat meatballs on bread? Then make a hot sub sandwich using some fresh Italian or French bread. Look at the Hot Meatball Sub recipe in this book.

That should hit the spot for you sandwich lovers if you love sandwiches like I do.

MUSHROOM RISOTTO

Serves: 4
Level: Easy
Needed: 1 medium saucepan, 1 large skillet or frying pan

INGREDIENTS

6 cups chicken broth
3 TBSP olive oil (divided)
1 pound Portobello mushrooms (thinly sliced)
3/4 lb white mushrooms (thinly sliced)
2 shallots (diced)
1 + 1/2 cups Arborio rice
1/2 cup dry white wine
Sea salt to taste
Black pepper (freshly ground) to taste
3 TBSP finely chopped chives
4 TBSP butter (either salted or unsalted)
1/3 cup Parmesan cheese (freshly grated)

DIRECTIONS

1. In a sauce pot, warm the broth over low heat (approx 4 to 5 mins) and then turn off the heat.

2. In a separate large frying pan, heat 2 TBSP of olive oil over medium heat (for about 15 seconds) and stir in both types of mushrooms, and cook until soft (approx 5 mins).

3. Remove mushrooms along with their liquid, and put into a bowl setting it aside for later.

4. Using the same pan on low heat, add 1 more TBSP olive oil and stir in the shallots, cooking them for about 1 or 2 minutes while stirring.

5. Add rice to frying pan with the shallots stirring constantly to coat the rice with oil for about 2 minutes until some of the oil is absorbed.

6. When the rice has changed to a pale color pour in wine and stir constantly, until fully absorbed.

7. Next add 1/2 cup of the chicken broth to the rice, and stir until the broth is absorbed.

8. Continue adding 1/2 cup of broth at a time, stirring continually, until the liquid is absorbed and the rice is "al dente" (98% cooked) for approx 15 to 20 minutes.

9. When all of the broth is gone, "or" the rice is cooked to al dente, you can stop adding the broth.

10. By tasting the rice you'll know when the texture is perfect and you can stop cooking. Just make sure that it's not too undercooked, but al dente instead, and then turn off the heat.

11. Immediately stir in mushrooms with liquid, butter, chives, parmesan, mix well (1 min) and taste.

12. You can turn on the heat for one more minute if the rice needs just a little more cooking but turn off the heat after a minute.

13. Season with salt and pepper and enjoy while it's still warm with your favorite beverage.

TIPS & NOTES

A glass of white wine or a martini is perfect with the risotto.

Don't forget fresh bread and butter. Bread By adding some olives on the side can offer a nice touch so use your imagination.

CHICKEN MARSALA

Serves: 4
Level: Medium

INGREDIENTS

4 Chicken breasts (skinless, boneless) approx 1 + 1/2 pounds
All-purpose flour (for dredging)
Sea Salt or kosher salt
Ground black pepper
1/4 cup extra-virgin olive oil
8 oz Cremini or Porcini mushrooms (stems removed and halved)
1/2 cup sweet Marsala wine
1/2 cup chicken stock
2 TBSP unsalted butter
1/4 cup chopped flat-leaf parsley
2 TBSP water

DIRECTIONS

1. Place plastic wrap on top of a cutting board or counter to protect it from bacteria.

2. Place the chicken breasts side by side on top of the plastic wrap and then place another layer of plastic wrap on top of them and cover them.

3. Now pound with a flat meat mallet or something similar until they're approx 1/4 inch thick. And remove the top layer of plastic wrap and discard.

4. Put some flour in a shallow bowl or dish and season with some salt and pepper; mix with a fork.

5. Heat the oil over medium-high flame in a large skillet.

6. While oil is heating, dredge both sides of the chicken in the seasoned flour (shake off the excess).

7. Carefully place the chicken into the pan (without splattering the hot oil).

8. Fry for 1 or 2 minutes on each side or until a light golden color, turning once. Don't over-cook.

9. After the chicken is cooked, remove it to a large plate.

10. Lower the heat of the pan to medium-low, add the mushrooms, and about 2 TBSP water.

11. Sauté until they're nicely browned and their moisture has evaporated (approx 5 minutes).

12. Season mushrooms with salt, pepper, and pour wine into the pan, boiling for about 30 seconds.

13. Add the chicken stock and simmer for a minute to reduce and thicken the sauce slightly.

14. Stir in the butter and melt it. Then return the chicken to the pan, simmering for about 1 minute.

15. After the liquid penetrates the chicken on both sides and is heated through turn off the heat.

16. Garnish with chopped parsley and serve. Enjoy this restaurant quality meal.

TIPS

Serve this chicken dish with a baked potato, rice or pasta on the side. A glass of wine too.

You can use Madeira wine instead of Marsala wine if you can't find any.
It's delicious too and many restaurants use this type of wine and rename the dish to Madeira.

ANGEL HAIR PASTA with PESTO

Serves: 4
Level: Easy

INGREDIENTS

1 lb of pasta (either: Angel Hair, Capellini or any thin low number pasta)
2 cups fresh basil (leaves only and packed down)
1/2 cup pine nuts (un-toasted)
1/2 cup extra-virgin olive oil
1/2 cup Parmesan cheese (use freshly grated "Parmigiano-Reggiano" cheese only!)
2 large garlic cloves
1/4 tsp sea salt (Finely ground Himalayan salt or any quality salt can be used for this recipe)
Black pepper (freshly ground fine powder)
1 TBSP clean water (purified or distilled)
1 TBSP fresh squeezed lemon juice (fresh juice is always preferred but if using reconstituted lemon juice then only 1 teaspoon is needed)
(Option) Add 1/2 cup of fresh parsley tops if you like the flavor of parsley
(Option) Add a TBSP of Romano cheese for a little extra tangy flavor

DIRECTIONS (Making the Pesto Sauce)

1. Just before you cook the pasta, make the sauce.

2. Combine the basil, pine nuts, garlic, and olive oil in a food processor or blender and blend until it becomes a puree. If adding parsley you can add it now also.

3. Scrape down the sides and add the water with lemon juice. Blend for 10 seconds.

4. Add the cheese, salt and pepper to taste, and blend again until blended together. If adding Romano cheese you can add it now also. Do not over blend.

5. Scrape the sides and blend again for a few more seconds.

6. This pesto can now be added to the pasta and toss.

7. Drizzle a little more extra virgin olive oil on top and serve.

DIRECTIONS (Making the Pasta)

1. Bring a large pot of salted water to a boil.

2. Cook pasta according to the directions or for about 3 to 5 mins until al dente (98% cooked).

3. Drain the pasta well and transfer to a bowl.

4. Immediately mix with presto sauce or a little olive oil to prevent sticking.

NOTE

You can serve this dish at room temperature or even cold if you like.

PENNE ALLA VODKA

Serves: 4
Level: Easy

INGREDIENTS

1 lb of penne pasta
4 TBSP of great tasting olive oil
1 medium yellow onion (chopped)
2 large cloves of garlic (minced)
1/2 teaspoon crushed red pepper flakes (seeds always removed preferred)
1 tsp dried oregano
1 cup vodka
2 (28-ounce) cans Italian peeled plum tomatoes or puree
2 tsp Sea salt or kosher salt
2 pinches of fresh ground black pepper powder
1 cup heavy cream
1/2 cup Parmesan cheese (freshly grated)
3 TBSP fresh oregano (optional)

DIRECTIONS

1. In a large sauce pan heat the olive oil over medium heat.

2. Add the onions and garlic, stirring every minute until translucent (approx 3 mins).

3. Add the red pepper flakes with dried oregano and stir for approx 1 minute.

4. Add vodka to the pan and continue cooking until reduced to about half the volume (2 minutes).

5. While vodka's reducing cut off any hard little green spots on the top of tomatoes where the stem was attached and crush with your hands squeezing over a bowl then add the tomatoes into the pan.

6. Add 2 tsp salt, a pinch of black pepper, stir then cover and cook on lowest heat (approx 45 mins).

7. Taste the sauce. If it's to your satisfaction then go to the next step, if not then cook longer.

8. Turn off the heat of the saucepan.

9. In a separate large pot, boil water with a few TBSP of salt and cook the pasta until al dente.

10. Drain and lightly rinse to stop the cooking. Set aside and let all of the water drain off.

11. Place the tomato mixture in a blender or use a hand blender directly into the sauce pan (preferred) and blend until the sauce is a smooth puree (approx 30-60 seconds).

12. If you prefer small chunky pieces in the sauce you can skip the blending step above.

13. Start to reheat the sauce over low heat.

14. Add 2 tsp fresh oregano (optional).

15. Slowly pour in the heavy cream to the tomato sauce while constantly mixing until the sauce becomes a creamy consistency, and a medium to light orange color.

16. Add salt and pepper to taste.

17. Simmer on low for approx 2 to 3 minutes to blend all of the flavors.

18. Toss the pasta into sauce and heat for about 1or 2 minutes then stir in 1/2 cup of Parmesan cheese.

19. Serve with an additional sprinkle of Parmesan or your favorite grated cheese on the table.

Optional: Garnish with fresh parsley.

20. Of course by now you know I'm going to say to enjoy this with fresh bread and butter.

CHICKEN PICCATA

Serves 2
Level: Easy
Needed: a Stainless Steel Pan and a Metal Whisk

INGREDIENTS

2 skinless and boneless chicken breasts (butter-flied and then cut in half)
2 cups of all-purpose flour (for dredging)
Sea salt (to taste)
Black pepper (to taste)
6 TBSP unsalted butter
5 TBSP cooking oil (either pure olive oil or sunflower oil)
1/3 cup fresh lemon juice
1/2 cup chicken stock
1/4 cup brined capers (rinsed)
1/3 cup fresh parsley (chopped)

DIRECTIONS

1. Season the chicken with salt and pepper, then dredge the chicken in flour on both sides and shake off the excess flour.

2. In a large skillet over medium high heat, melt 2 TBSP of butter along with 3 TBSP cooking oil.

3. As soon as butter and oil begin to sizzle, immediately add half of the chicken (2 pieces) and cook for 2 to 3 minutes.

4. When the chicken is lightly browned on the bottom (check by lifting), then flip and cook the other side for an additional 2 minutes.

5. Remove and transfer to plate.

6. Add and melt 2 more TBSP butter along with a couple more TBSP of oil.

7. When butter and oil start to lightly sizzle, add the rest of the chicken (2 pieces) and repeat the process by browning both sides as you did earlier.

8. Remove "only" the chicken from pan and transfer it to a plate.

9. Remove the pan from the heat and reduce the heat to very low. (Immediately go to step 10).

10. Into the pan add the lemon juice, chicken stock and capers.

11. Return the pan to heat and bring to boil.

12. Scrape and mix the cooked brown pieces from the pan for extra flavor.

13. Do a quality check by tasting for amount of seasoning needed.

14. Return all chicken to the pan and simmer for about 2 to 3 minutes, allowing everything simmer together. Making sure the chicken is totally cooked by tasting. Do not overcook.

15. Remove chicken to a plate or platter.

16. Add the remaining 2 TBSP of butter to sauce and whisk until blended.

17. Pour sauce over chicken and garnish with parsley or your choice of garnish.

18. Enjoy this tasty lemon chicken dish with everything else you'd love it add to your plate.

HOT SUB SANDWICHES
CHICKEN PARMESAN SUB

Level Super Easy

Feeds: 2 people (per large loaf of Italian bread)

One of my favorite all time sandwiches!

The first thing you'll need to make this sandwich cooked Chicken Parmesan. You can get the recipe right in this book and then just follow the easy directions below.

DIRECTIONS

1. Preheat the oven for about 10 minutes to approx 375 degrees F. Or you can use a large toaster oven instead but be careful this can get messy.

2. Slice the loaf in half the long way.

Option: You can even use the recipe called Mazzo's Garlic Bread from this book if you'd like a super garlicy tasting sandwich? If you'd like to try this then make the bread from that recipe but first you'll need to make the Chicken Parmesan and then place it on the bread with a little extra cheese and sauce and let it all melt together in the oven. If you want a more traditional Chicken Parm Sandwich then continue to follow the rest of the directions below.

3. Place some thinly sliced Mozzarella cheese over the bread.

4. Make the Chicken Parmesan from the recipe in this book and then cut as much chicken to fit on the bread as you want, then top it with extra Mozzarella cheese.

5. Sprinkle some freshly grated Parmesan or Romano cheese on top, or a combo of both cheeses, if you're in the mood for a little sharper flavor.

6. Spoon on several tablespoons of tomato sauce over the chicken. Not too much though the bread will get soggy. If you want more sauce you can always add it later to the sandwich.

7. Next, place more Mozzarella cheese over the top of chicken.

8. Place this super loaded sandwich into the oven for a few minutes until the cheese has melted. If using a broiler, only leave it in for 1 or 2 minutes or the bread can burn!

9. Remove carefully from oven or toaster oven.

10. Wait a minute for it to cool a bit, then cut in half and enjoy your gourmet sandwich.

This sandwich goes well with your favorite carbonated soft drink.

HOT MEATBALL PARMESAN SUB

Level: Super Easy
Feeds: 2 people (per large loaf of Italian bread)

Want to make a hot meatball sub sandwich that tastes so much better than ones served in restaurants?

Then make this one. This is one of my favorite hot sandwiches and it also ranks in the top 3 most famous hot Italian sub sandwiches.

For this one you'll need to make the meatballs from the Meatballs and Tomato Sauce recipe in this book then follow the directions below.

DIRECTIONS

1. Preheat the oven for about 10 minutes to approx 375 degrees F. Or you can use a very large toaster oven instead but be careful this can get messy also.

2. Slice the loaf in half the long way.

OPTION: You can use the recipe from Mazzo's Garlic Bread if you want a fantastic garlicy, flavored sub. If choosing the garlic bread just place a few meatballs cut in half, into the garlic bread and top with sauce and cheese then melt everything together. For the traditional sandwich follow the directions below.

3. Place some thinly sliced Mozzarella cheese over the bread.

4. Cut as many meatballs in half as you would like eat, and place them flat side down onto the bread pushing them into the cheese.

5. Sprinkle some grated fresh Parmesan or Romano cheese over the meatballs or a combo of both.

6. Spoon on several tablespoons of tomato sauce over the meatballs. Not too much though.

7. Next, put some more Mozzarella cheese over the top of the meatballs.

8. Place the loaded sandwich into the oven for a few minutes until the cheese has melted. If using a broiler leave it in for a minute or 2 but not so long or the bead burns fast.

9. Remove the sandwich after the cheese has melted.

10. Wait 2 minutes, then cut with in half and enjoy your gourmet meatball sandwich.

EGGPLANT PARMESAN SUB

Level: Super Easy

Feeds: 2 people (per large loaf of Italian bread)

Another one of my favorite sandwiches is Eggplant Parm.

So many others like it too but not as many as the other two sandwiches in this book unfortunately.

This sandwich is lighter than the other two meat sandwiches but is so tasty as long as you make fry the eggplant until it is soft and tender.

But no worries because I gave you an incredibly tasty Eggplant Parm Recipe in this book so use it to make the best hot sub sandwich you've ever had. Now just follow the easy directions below.

DIRECTIONS

1. Preheat the oven to approx 375 degrees F for 10 minutes or can use a large toaster oven instead for a quicker recipe without having to pre-heat it.

2. Slice the loaf in half the long way.

3. Place some thinly sliced Mozzarella cheese over the bread.

4. Make the Eggplant Parm Recipe in this book then take a few pieces of the eggplant and place them onto the bread, on top of the cheese.

5. Sprinkle some grated or fresh Parmesan or Romano cheese over the eggplant.

6. Then spoon on several tablespoons of tomato sauce over the Eggplant. Not too much. If you want more sauce you can always add it later to the sandwich.

7. Next, put some more Mozzarella cheese over the top of Eggplant.

8. Place this super loaded sandwich into the oven for a few minutes until the cheese has melted. If using a broiler, only leave it in for 1 or 2 minutes or the bread can burn.

9. Remove the sandwich from the oven.

10. Wait 1-2 minutes, then cut in half and enjoy your delicious Eggplant Parm sandwich.

DESSERT RECIPES
GELATO

The difference between Gelato and ice cream is that Gelato has a lower fat content due its higher ratio of milk to cream. Also with the air volume being less, it makes this dessert denser and creamier than ice cream. Skipping the vanilla as an ingredient makes this an authentic Italian treat called Gelato di Crema.

Removing the eggs from this recipe or increasing the amount of cream to a higher ratio would turn this into what you know as ice cream instead.

Your ice cream maker may cause this recipe to be a little on the icy side as opposed to the creamy side because it most likely churns the milk and cream faster, creating more air than a typical Italian Gelato machine would.

You may want to try to making this the authentic way not using vanilla the first time. Later you can have fun and experiment a little with this recipe by playing around with the ingredients, and learn how the variations affect the taste. I'm giving you the ingredients below for a Famous Gelato recipe.

You can experiment later by changing the flavor after you are happy with the regular flavor. When skipping the eggs you don't have to cook the milk, but you may still want to warm it up a little, just so the sugar can melt easily.

Without adding the eggs the flavor will change and taste a lot lighter. Want to know how to transform this simple Gelato into other flavors? It's so simple. Who knows you may turn into the next Ben or Jerry.

Makes Approximately 1 Quart or (30-32 oz)
Level: Easy

INGREDIENTS

2 cups milk
1 cup heavy cream
3 egg yolks
1/2 cup sugar
Option: 1 tsp of real vanilla extract

DIRECTIONS

1. In a medium saucepan, mix the milk with cream.
2. Warm it until some foam forms around the edges.
3. Remove the pan from heat.
4. In a large bowl, beat the egg yolks and sugar until airy.
5. Pour the warm milk gradually and slowly into the egg yolk mixture bowl while whisking constantly.
6. Now return the mixture to saucepan.
7. Cook over medium heat while stirring with a wooden spoon constantly until the mixture starts to coat the back of the spoon and liquid begins to gel without any little egg lumps. If you see any egg lumps form then remove the pan from heat immediately.
8. Pour the mixture through a fine strainer or a sieve into a bowl.
9. Cover the bowl and chill it for several hours or even overnight.
10. Pour the mixture into an ice cream maker, and follow the ice cream maker's manufacturer's instructions.
11. Transfer to a sealed container, and freeze until it becomes firm. If the gelato becomes too firm you can always place it in the refrigerator instead until you're happy with the consistency.
12. Mix with a spoon and serve into your favorite cup or bowl.

ALMOND BISCOTTI

Makes: approx: 24 cookies
Level: Intermediate

INGREDIENTS

3 cups all-purpose flour
1 + 1/2 cups sugar
1/8 tsp salt
1 tsp pure vanilla extract
1 tsp pure almond extract
1 tsp baking powder
5 eggs
1 + 1/2 cups almonds (non-salted, roasted)

DIRECTIONS

1. Pre-heat an oven to 350 degrees F.

2. Take 1 of the 5 eggs & separate 1 egg white placing it aside in a cup

3. In large bowl beat the 4 eggs plus the yolk of 5th egg.

4. Add the sugar to the beaten eggs along with the vanilla and almond extract.

5. Whisk together for a couple minutes until the sugar is dissolved into the eggs with no graininess.

6. In a separate large mixing bowl, mix the dry ingredients (flour, baking powder, and salt) using large spoon, then pour the wet ingredients into the dry and mix well until you get a wet doughy mixture.

7. Mix with either with a large wooden spoon or by hand (approx 3 mins).

8. Chop the almonds into pieces. Not too small, but basically each almond should be broken into 4 pieces.

9. You can also use slivered or sliced almonds. They are an ideal shape (visually) for this recipe but not important for taste.

10. Mix almonds thoroughly into the dough with a large mixing spoon.

11. Divide the dough into 2 balls.

12. Sprinkle flour on counter surface and hands to prevent dough from sticking.

13. With your hands, roll the balls (one at a time) into 2 logs (approx 2 inches high x 11 inches long).

14. Place the two logs onto a baking sheet lined with parchment paper.

15. Now add approx 2 ounces of water to the egg white and beat for 15 seconds with a fork.

16. Brush using your fingers or a brush to spread the egg mixture lightly on the top and sides of each log to give a nice shine while baking.

17. Place the tray into the preheated 350 degree F oven and bake for between 18-28 minutes or until the tops are browned (not burnt).

18. Take the tray out and cool for (approx 10 mins) so you can handle the logs without burning your hands.

19. Do not turn the oven off. You'll need to finish baking these to make them crispy in the center.

20. Pick up one log at a time and place onto a large plate.

21. Using a sharp knife cut the end pieces off. You can eat the ends if you wish.

22. Carefully slice the cookie loafs using a sharp knife into approx ½ inch slices without them crumbling when slicing. Don't press down hard while slicing!

23. Lay the slices flat side down on a baking tray and place into a 350 degree F oven for about 15 minutes until crispy in the center also. You can add a couple more minutes baking if the center doesn't look done.

24. Option: sprinkle some powdered sugar on cookies and enjoy your cookies dunked into your favorite hot beverage.

PANNA COTTA

Makes: 6 servings
Level: Intermediate

INGREDIENTS

1/4 cup milk
1 envelope unflavored gelatin (0.25 oz size)
2 + 1/2 cups heavy cream
1/2 cup white sugar (organic preferred)
1 fresh vanilla bean pod (or) 1+1/2 tsp liquid vanilla extract

DIRECTIONS

1. In a small bowl pour only the milk and stir in the gelatin powder.

2. In a separate saucepan, stir the heavy cream and sugar together, and then place the saucepan over medium heat.

3. Bring the heavy cream and sugar to a full boil and "immediately" reduce the heat to low.

4. Keep an eye on this, as the cream will rise rapidly to the top of the pan.

5. Now pour the gelatin and milk mixture into the hot cream.

6. Stir until completely dissolved.

7. Add the vanilla liquid extract (or) if using a fresh vanilla bean slice it open the long way.

8. Scrape the inside with the back of a knife to remove all the seeds and add them along with the whole bean to the pan with the hot cream.

9. Cook for one minute, while constantly stirring.

10. Remove the pan from the heat, and let it sit for 5 minutes then give a good stir.

11. Take out the vanilla bean pod empty shell.

12. Pour into six individual ramekin dishes or as many small dessert cups as you wish.

13. Cool the ramekins or dishes while uncovered at room temperature.

14. After they've cooled, cover with plastic wrap

15. Refrigerate for at least 5 hours (preferably overnight before serving).

RAINBOW COOKIES

Makes: Lots of cookies
Level: Intermediate

INGREDIENTS

2 cups of flour
4 eggs yolks
4 egg whites
1 cup of sugar
2 sticks butter (at room temperature)
Apricot jam (large jar)
3/4 lb almond paste
4 oz. chocolate (semi-sweet baker's chocolate)
Green and red food color

DIRECTIONS

1. In a stand mixer add the egg "yolks" and butter. Mix well then Add the sugar and mix again.

2. Break the almond paste into small pieces before adding to the mixer. Add to mixer and mix well, then add the flour to the mixer, and mix well again.

3. In a separate bowl, beat the egg whites (with a fork) until they become a little foamy.

4. Add them to the mixer. Mix thoroughly for a few minutes until the dough looks soft and smooth.

5. Divide it into 3 equal parts and place into three separate bowls.

6. The dough in the first bowl should be left alone and no color is needed. It will stay white.

7. The dough in the second bowl you'll color green by adding 3 drops of green color and mix well.

8. The dough in the third bowl you'll color red by adding 3 drops of red color and mix well.

9. You can add a couple more drops if you prefer to create a deeper color but it's not unnecessary.

10. Evenly spread the mixes in three separate ungreased aluminum baking sheets of 12 x 8 inches each. They must all be the same size.

11. Bake them each at 375 F degrees for 10 -12 mins. Then let them all cool.

12. Place a piece of parchment paper on a large wooden cutting board.

13. Remove and place the green sheet cake on top of the paper.

14. Spread a thin layer of apricot jam evenly over the entire top surface of the green sheet cake.

15. Next, place the white sheet cake on top of the green sheet and spread the apricot jam again on the white surface just as you have done to the green cake.

16. Take the final red sheet cake, place it over the white. Don't spread jam on the top of red layer.

17. With a large flat spatula or your hands press the top layer firmly to make all the three layers stick

18. With a sharp serrated knife trim all four edges of the combined cakes.

19. Melt the chocolate and spread half of it over the top of the red layer sheet cake only.

20. Let the chocolate totally dry, preferably overnight.

21. Now you can finish adding the chocolate to the bottom of the cake by turning it upside down and spread melted chocolate over the other side also.

22. Let the chocolate dry again.

23. Cut the cake into cookie squares of approx 1+1/2" x 3/4" or any size that you desire and enjoy!

NOTE: For the health conscious maybe you can find a natural color instead of the regular food dyes.

LIMONCELLO BABA

Makes: Several Servings
Level: Intermediate

NOTE

Refrigerate the flour for at least 2 hours before using

INGREDIENTS (for the Baba Batter)

1 pound flour (all purpose or cake flour) See notes at the end for cup measurements
9 eggs (cold, straight from the refrigerator)
1/2 TBSP salt (sea salt preferred)
2 + 1/4 TBSP sugar
1 + 1/2 TBSP water
4 + 1/4 oz unsalted butter divided into 10 pieces (room temperature)
1 TBSP fresh yeast

INGREDIENTS (for the Limoncello Syrup)

3 cups water
1 cup sugar (organic preferred)
The juice of one lemon
The peel of one lemon (grated or zest)
1 + 1/2 cups Limoncello liquor (Limoncello is definitely preferred but you can use dark rum)
Lemon marmalade for brushing each Baba and give then a shiny appearance

DIRECTIONS (Making the Baba)

1. In a small bowl, add the water and melt the yeast into the water.

2. Add 4 TBSP of the flour and mix to form a small ball of dough.

3. Cover the bowl containing the dough and place it in a warm location of the house so it will rise.

4. When the dough doubles in volume the rising has finished (approx 40 mins).

5. In a stand mixer, add the small ball of dough and the remaining 1 pound of flour.

6. Start the mixer using the paddle attachment.

7. In a separate large bowl, crack and add all of the eggs. Break each of the yolks with a fork.

8. As the flour is mixing add the eggs a little bit at a time.

9. Add the sugar.

10. Set the speed at position #2 and continue to mix for about 20 mins.

11. The dough will become very elastic and it will get completely stuck to the paddle.

12. Remove all the dough from the paddle.

13. Replace the paddle with the dough hook.

14. Start the mixer again with the dough inside.

15. Dip the pieces of butter into the salt.

16. Add the pieces of butter one by one. Wait until the previous piece has been absorbed into the dough before adding the next.

17. Add the remaining salt and continue to mix at the #2 speed for another 15 minutes approximately.

18. The dough will become soft, elastic and slightly dark when it's finished being mixed.

19. Clean the dough off the hook.

20. With a spatula scrape all the dough "to the center" of the bowl.

21. Cover the mixing bowl and place it in the warm part of the house for approx 3 hours or until the dough has doubled in size.

22. When the dough has doubled in size or 3 hours have passed get the Baba molds ready.

23. Take each Baba mold and butter the inside using your finger.

24. Next take each Baba mold and sprinkle with flour. This will help the dough not to stick while baking.

25. Take some dough in your hand, squeeze letting the dough come out. Drop the dough in each mold filling the molds approx a little more than the halfway mark.

26. Preheat the oven at 350F.

27. After all the dough is in the Baba molds, cover the molds with a towel or plastic wrap and place them in the warm location to rise again.

28. After about 30 minutes the dough will reach the top of the mold and you are ready to bake.

29. Bake the Baba for (approx 30 mins) checking the color. All ovens vary in temperature just a little. Take them out when they are "golden" brown.

30. Let them cool and you are ready to dip them in the Limoncello syrup.

DIRECTIONS (Making the syrup)

1. Put the 3 cups of water and 1 cup of sugar in a pot together

2. Turn on the heat.

3. Add the juice of one lemon and the zest of one lemon peel.

4. After it comes to a steady boil, shut it off to let it cool.

5. After its cold, add the Limoncello and mix.

6. Dip the Baba submerging it into the syrup for a few minutes each so they will absorb the syrup.

7. When they soaked up plenty of the syrup and they are shiny appearance, brush them with lemon marmalade or any other clear type of marmalade that you have.

8. They can be served as is or filled with any type of cream that you desire.

9. Refrigerate and serve cold then enjoy these great Babas.

You can find Baba Molds on the kitchen tools page of my site at mariomazzo.com/kitchen-tools

Turn off your pop up blocker before going to the kitchen tools page or you won't see all of the great pictures of the tools and gadgets.

RICOTTA CHEESECAKE

Serves: 8-12
Level: Easy

INGREDIENTS (for the Crust)

1 egg
2 oz milk
2 oz butter or (half of a stick) melted
2 oz sugar (organic)
1 TBSP baking powder
4 cups of flour (or as much needed to make the dough firm)

INGREDIENTS (for the Filling)

Ricotta cheese (2 pounds or two 15 oz containers)
6 eggs
1 cup sugar
1 tsp vanilla
1/2 TBSP lemon zest
1/2 TBSP orange zest
Optional 1 oz orange juice (fresh squeezed)

DIRECTIONS (Making the Crust)

1. In a large bowl add the egg and whisk (15 sec).

2. Add sugar whisk (45 sec).

3. Add milk and whisk (15 sec).

4. Add butter and whisk (20 sec).

5. Add baking powder and whisk (15 sec).

6. Start to add the flour (only about a cup at a time) and mix well with your hands, until all the ingredients are well blended. You might not need all of the 4 cups flour for the dough.

7. Place the dough on a flat surface and continue to working the dough with your hands adding flour as needed until it reaches a firm consistency.

8. Make a round ball with the dough and flatten by hand into a round shape.

9. Sprinkle the top of the dough with flour.

10. Use a rolling pin to flatten the dough into a round circle thin enough until it becomes approx 1/4 inch thick.

11. Make sure that the size of dough is about 15" in diameter.

12. Take a 9 inch "Spring Form Pan" and coat the bottom and sides generously with butter.

13. Now sprinkle a good amount of flour to coat the buttered pan, lifting the pan and shaking / while turning with your hands until the flour gets distributed around the pan and coats the butter.

14. Place the dough over the pan. Let any excess dough hang over the sides of the pan. This will be your pie crust.

15. Do "not" cut the excess until later (see the steps below).

DIRECTIONS (Making the Filling)

1. In a large mixing bowl add all the ingredients for the filling (see 2nd ingredient list above).

2. Mix all the ingredients using an electric mixer.

3. Now assemble the cake by pouring the filling into the baking pan over the dough.

4. With a sharp knife cut any excess dough.

5. Use caution when cutting the excess dough leaving about 1 inch of extra dough above the surface of the ricotta filling.

6. Bake for approx 90 minutes at 350F.

7. Top with confectioner's (powdered) sugar or add any toppings you like.

8. Let cool to become firm before serving then enjoy this delicious cake.

TIRAMISU

Makes: 6 servings
Level: Easy

INGREDIENTS

6 egg yolks
1 cup sugar (organic)
1 + 1/4 cup mascarpone cream cheese
1 + 3/4 cup heavy whipping cream
14 oz "Italian Lady Finger Cookies"
1 cup cold espresso coffee
1 TBSP cocoa powder for dusting
Optional 1/4 cup coffee flavored liquor

DIRECTIONS

1. Make the sabayon (which is the cream) by combining egg yolks and sugar in the top of a double boiler, over boiling water.

2. Reduce the heat to low, and cook for approx 10 minutes, stirring constantly.

3. Remove from the heat and whip the mixture until it thickens and is a lemon color.

4. Add the Mascarpone cream cheese to whipped egg yolk mixture and beat until combined.

5. In a separate bowl, whip the heavy whipping cream until stiff peaks form.

6. Next, gently fold the whipped cream into the mascarpone sabayon mixture and set aside.

7. Mix the cold espresso with the coffee liquor and dip the lady fingers into the mixture just long enough to get them wet. DO NOT soak them or leave them in too long!

8. Arrange the lady fingers in the bottom of a 9 inch square baking dish.

9. Spoon half the mascarpone cream filling over the lady fingers.

10. Repeat process with another layer of lady fingers and cream (making a double layer).

11. Refrigerate at least 3-4 hours.

12. Dust with cocoa powder before serving.

13. Enjoy this famous Italian recipe with your favorite beverage.

CANNOLI

Makes: Approx 20 Cannoli
Level: Easy or Advanced (depending on if you are making the shells yourself or not)

*Special kitchen tools and gadgets needed: **Cannoli molds** and a rolling pin. If making the Cannoli shells yourself and you don't have the molds yet needed for this recipe.

They aren't expensive and you can purchase them through the links on my website at mariomazzo.com/kitchen-tools
I'm an Amazon affiliate.
Or you can visit a great Cannoli website that has lots of Cannoli products by visiting www.CannoliKingdom.com
*You can skip totally skip buying the molds and a rolling pin if you are buying the shells instead pre-made from a store that sells them.
The shells are also on my site if skipping making them yourself. They are also available on www.CannoliKingdom.com
Or use good mini ice cream sugar cones to save yourself a lot of work and time.
See Your Options in the Options & Tips Section in this Recipe.

INGREDIENTS (for Making the Shells)

FOR THE DEEP FRYING

1 quart (or liter) approx of Safflower or Sunflower Oil (for deep frying the shells) Exact amount depends on your pot size

FOR MAKING THE DOUGH

2 cups all-purpose flour
1 TBSP granulated sugar
1/4 tsp sea salt
1 TBSP plus 2 tsp unsalted butter, cut into small pieces
1 egg yolk
1/2 cup dry white wine
Extra flour for rolling
Extra Powdered sugar (for dusting when finished)
If you choose to skip making the Cannoli shells, the only ingredients required are those for making the crème filling which is very simple to do.

OPTIONS & TIPS

You can skip buying the Cannoli molds and buy the Cannoli shells pre made instead. You can also purchase the shells online and have them shipped to your house, but I've heard stories that sometimes they arrive broken due to vibrations during shipping. But you do have plenty of options.

You may want to make the cream first and try it inside mini ice cream cones the first time to get the hang of making the cream before shopping for shells or the molds to make them.

Buying the shells from a store or bakery will save you lots of time and the effort that goes into making these deep fried shells. A local Italian bakery that makes Cannoli should be able to sell you several shells. If having an authentic Cannoli shell isn't too important to you, then some waffle or sugar cones may do the trick and may be tasty. Now of course the flavor and texture will be different, but with delicious cream it may not matter that much to you. So you can decide what's best for you.

INGREDIENTS (for Making the Crème Filling)

2 cups ricotta cheese (Impastata Ricotta Cheese Preferred if available) otherwise use whole milk small curd type drained
1/3 cup organic white sugar (granulated)
1/3 cup powdered sugar
2 TBSP cream cheese
1/2 tsp vanilla extract
1/4 tsp ground cinnamon powder
1/3 cup mini semisweet chocolate chips
1 small fresh lemon (washed and rinsed well)
1 egg, lightly beaten, for egg wash

DIRECTIONS (for Making the Shells)

* You can skip the following 7 steps if you already purchased the shells

1. In a medium bowl, sift together the flour, sugar and salt.
2. Work the butter pieces into the flour with your fingers until the mixture becomes coarse and sandy.
3. Add the egg yolk and the white wine and mix until the dough becomes smooth.
4. Spread a piece of plastic wrap on a flat surface and place the dough in the center.
5. Wrap the plastic loosely around it and press the dough to fill the gap.
6. Flattening the dough will mean less rolling later.
7. Let it rest in the fridge for a few minutes while you make the filling.

DIRECTIONS (for Making the Crème Filling)

1. Before you start, drain the ricotta (if you can't find the Impastata Ricotta cheese) using a strainer and a large pot under it to catch all the excess liquid to be removed (for approx 1 hour).
2. Do not let the liquid touch the bottom of the ricotta while draining.
3. After the ricotta has been drained place it into a very dry large mixing bowl and whisk until smooth.
4. Add both sugars, cinnamon and vanilla extract.
5. Mix well with a spoon and then whisk until all of the ingredients are blended well until all of the grains of sugar are dissolved.
6. Add the 2 TBSP of cream cheese and blend in by hand using a whisk or an electric mixer.
7. Stir in the mini chocolate chips.
8. Lightly zest the exterior of half or all of the lemon and stir it into the ricotta.
9. Refrigerate for 1 hour before using.
10. Give a quick stir and then it can be used to fill the inside of the shells.

DIRECTIONS (for Rolling and Frying the Shells)

* You can skip the section for frying the shells if you have already bought some shells or another type of crunchy body for putting the crème into.

This step involves deep frying in very hot oil. You should be extremely careful and have some experience with hot frying oil for this step. If not please buy pre-made shells. You can find them at local bakeries or search online.

1. In a medium pot with a heavy bottom, heat the oil to 375 degrees F. Use a cooking thermometer placed into the oil.

2. While the oil in the pot is heating, sift an even layer of flour on a flat surface and flour a rolling pin.

3. Roll the dough until it is very thin (about 1/8-inch thick) and cut into fourths. Work in small batches.

4. Find any glass, small bowl, or cookie cutter that has a 3 to 4 inch diameter and cut rounds by tracing each one with a knife to assure dough has been fully cut (approx 20 circles)

5. Wrap each circle around a Cannoli mold and press down where the edges meet.

6. Use some of the egg wash where edges meet to seal and shut by pressing down on the edge to secure.

7. Keep the edges near the ends of the mold slightly loose to allow the oil to enter to fry them evenly.

8. Use a pair of tongs to hold the edge of the bare metal part of the mold.

9. Submerge gently into hot oil and fry until crispy (approx 2 to 3 mins). See the color turn to tan.

10. Remove the mold from the hot oil USING TONGS ONLY. Gently place down onto a plate or bowl.

11. Using a clean kitchen towel or a pair of clean thick unused yard or work gloves, carefully slide the shell off of the mold and set aside to cool for 15 minutes.

12. DO NOT fill with the cream until you are ready to eat the Cannoli. The shells can be stored in an airtight container for about 30 days.

13. Repeat the process until all of the shells are cooked.

DIRECTIONS (for Filling the Cannoli Shell with Crème)

1. Use a pastry bag (preferred) without a tip to pipe the ricotta into the Cannoli shells. If you don't have a bag then you can use an iced tea spoon or long butter knife.

2. Fill the Cannoli shells from both ends starting with piping the cream into the center of the shell first, then working your way to the ends.

3. Dust the outside of the shell with powdered sugar.

4. Serve immediately or within 10 minutes, or refrigerate for up to 10 minutes only. If you keep the crème in the shell too long it will begin to get soggy.

5. Make sure you serve your Cannoli crispy.

6. Before eating the Cannoli, don't forget to call me to tell me they're ready!

NOTES (for the Cannoli Shells)

Especially since there are lots of new chefs out there making this recipe I thought it's good for you to know you have an options. You can buy some pre-made Cannoli shells separately which is a whole lot easier.

The crème filling is very easy to make but the shells are much more difficult. The level to make the cream is easy but the shells are advanced.

A good option is to buy them at a local Italian Bakery or Italian Specialty Shop where you live. I never try to discourage someone from making the Cannoli shells, especially if capable of handling this task. Deep frying is not that difficult but caution should be taken.

The oil has to be at right around the perfect temperature within about 8 degrees either way, and is hot enough to cause a serious burn. Even a well-seasoned chef might prefer to run down to the local store and buy a dozen or two shells that are pre-made.

As for me, I'd prefer to find some delicious Cannoli shells sitting naked on the shelf at a store and buy them. Yes of course I love cooking but I'm not that into frying. It's time consuming and makes a mess. I'd prefer to use my time for other things like making a pizza, calzone, or baking something else.

I worked at a restaurant and made enough French fries for a lifetime, so now I just avoid it when possible and let others do frying for me. And always know, there are plenty of online video tutorials showing how to make the Cannoli shells. And finally, if you didn't know, one is a Cannolo and two or more are Cannoli.

HAPPY COOKING!

"Take pride in whatever you decide to create, but do it with excellence"

A Chef's Blessing To All Cooks!

May your recipes and food, along with everything in your life, turn out to be good and not bad.
May the food that you create, eat, and feed to others bring health and nourishment to your body, mind, soul and spirit!

Till next time Buon Appetito

Mario

PRODUCT RECOMMENDATIONS

I've chosen some high quality kitchen tools that you'll find on my website. Hopefully they'll make your kitchen chores easier. So check out some of them one day at mariomazzo.com/kitchen-tools

Also I'm a proud affiliate member of Amazon and of other quality companies that sell food and similar products online. Please show your support by initiating your browsing there.

When clicking on Amazon products there you'll be brought directly to Amazon's site. Thanks in advance for your support.

OTHER BOOKS by this AUTHOR

"Secret Ingredients"

This is a digital e-book and is available on my website for free download.

It's a mini book giving you some tips and tricks to make great tomato sauce and also an Asian flavored brown sauce.

More Great Cookbooks are Coming Shortly!

THANK YOU!

Thanks for purchasing my book
To show my appreciation I'd like to give you my Mini E-Book as a Gift

Download your copy of the digital e-book here at mariomazzo.com/free-book
And you'll be added to my free recipe club email list which gives you updates and other cool stuff.
GET MY MINI BOOK
SECRET INGREDIENTS FREE
USE THE 2 SECRET INGREDIENTS IN THIS BOOK TO MAKE 2 DELICIOUS SAUCES
TOMATO SAUCE RECIPE
ASIAN BROWN SAUCE RECIPE

"This is the first time I've given these recipes to anyone"

MARIO'S MINI AUTOBIOGRAPHY

I grew up in Brooklyn as a typical middle-class kid during the first 10 years of my life, then my parents moved away from the concrete jungle of New York into the Garden state New Jersey. For those of you that have never been to New Jersey it has some beautiful places, thus the name Garden State.

There are mountains on the west side, horse farms with fruit and vegetable farms in the center, and great beaches on the east. From central Jersey the trains can get you into New York City in less than an hour.

I still remember buying fresh baskets of tomatoes and bags of corn that were hand-picked minutes earlier from the fields. An old lady farmer that I frequently bought fresh corn from, one day made me taste an ear of fresh corn that was picked 10 minutes earlier. She told me to taste it raw and promised that it tasted as good as or better than when it's cooked. I thought she was crazy, but I was young and naïve back then.

She made a very bold claim that when it's fresh of the field it doesn't require cooking, because it's so sweet and tender. She then boasted about how she prefers to eat corn this way. She was a very nice hard working older woman that knew all about the corn she raised. Well guess what? She was right. I was surprised that it was so sweet, juicy and tender without being cooked. She made me a believer. Corn has changed a lot in the US since then. If I could get my hands on that corn again and that fresh, I'd probably eat it raw every day.

At a young age I learned what fresh fruit and veggies should taste like when grown in nutrient rich soil. The GM generation of food wasn't popular back then except for wheat, from what I've read. So everything tasted so much better back then.

When I moved from NJ when I was around 30 years old and since then I've lived in several places inside and outside the United States. I've seen some amazing things and also some crazy characters.

Growing up I cooked a lot, especially in my teen years especially in high school. My home economics teacher was a culinary grad from Le Cordon Bleu from what I recall. She taught us how to make some basic breakfast items like French toast, omelets, and other things like cookies and desserts. The best tasting of all these recipes which I made with my own hands was a homemade apple pie. At least when I brought it home that's what my mother told me. She said that it had the best crust she'd ever tasted.

Making this pie from scratch was fun but I never expected it to taste so delicious. It just goes to show you, that if you have a great traditional recipe, use quality ingredients, and follow basic directions, you can surprise yourself with something that may turn out to be an award winning dish!

In my younger days I loved learning about food until music took first place in my life. I practiced playing the drums many hours per week for a few years, and then became interested in art also. I've created many abstract paintings and believe that it's a great outlet for creativity.

Anyone can paint and you don't have to be good at it, just have fun. Most people I've talked to haven't tried painting but after they do they usually enjoy it. Two famous celebrities that I know of paint which are Jim Carey and Tony Bennett. Their art is beautiful and they happen to be very talented artists.

I started cooking more in my mid 20's and learned by watching the PBS TV famous chefs of that time. In the 1980's, PBS channels started airing lots of cooking shows with famous cooks such as Julia Child, Martin Yan and other fun chefs. There was this very funny guy, a Louisiana chef who made me laugh all the time. It was like watching a comedy cooking show. I forget his name but he was an old man who was fun to watch. I also loved watching Martin Yan cook up a storm and still do when I get a chance. This man really knows how to cook and even named his show "Yan Can Cook". He always made me laugh with his comical personality and I've learned some great tips from watching him.

About 10 years later cable television took over and started airing the various food network type channels with so many chefs from around the world that you never heard of. This created a desire for more people to learn how to cook at home instead of going to cooking school. TV can be a good thing.

Lots of these chefs became the famous celebrity chefs you're probably familiar with now like Emeril and the other Mario. Even though there's a multitude of TV chefs, you don't normally see authentic traditional recipes being cooked on their shows like you did in the earlier days of TV. This gave me an idea. Why not write classic cookbooks featuring traditional recipes and use only the best of the best 5 star recipes

I thought this would be a great benefit to home chefs and they wouldn't have to purchase many cookbooks just to get a couple dozen great classic recipes.

Getting back to my younger days, I got back into cooking and worked at couple of very humble little American family type restaurants. Unfortunately they weren't exciting enough for me and I quickly got bored. That's when I decided to attend Bartending School, and became a professional bartender.

I liked bartending but my planned bartending career was cut short. After several months of working as a bartender I was involved in what you would call a near fatal car wreck. I call it near fatal because I lived obviously.

I was hit head on by a drunk driver that who was travelling at an estimated speed of around 70 mph on the wrong side of the road. So please don't drink and drive. The kid that hit me was only 17 and under drinking age. He was on the wrong side of the road (mine) and was going so fast, that after hitting my car, his car flipped three times in the air. Sort of what you'd see in a movie.

After his car collided with mine, the rear end of my car was pointing up in the air leaning on the pole of a street sign. The front end of my car was compacted just like an aluminum can, ready to be recycled. The guy that hit me was driving a 57 Chevy that was all supped up and mine was a tiny little Opel Manta that I just bought 2 weeks earlier. If you know anything about cars you can see why this is a miracle that I survived, and without a scratch I must add.

I wasn't even wearing a seat belt. At the point of impact it felt as if there was no gravity. It was a very strange feeling. It felt like something was under me lifting me up in the air as the car hit me, sort of like an invisible buffer between my seat and my body. Like the loss of gravity when you drop from a rollercoaster or an amusement park ride. That type of impact would practically snap your head off your body, not make you feel like you're on a rollercoaster.

There weren't any seat belt laws in the early 80's in New Jersey. So we didn't get into the habit of clicking them when getting into a car. I did have some minor muscle trauma though in my lower back for a few months after this, so I had to take sedentary jobs and decided to quit bartending.

Even though I didn't get back into the food industry for a while, I've always remained in the kitchen cooking or baking after my back muscles felt better.

I liked baking and had much success with desserts. I quickly learned that most people love desserts as much as I do. I can't count how many fresh baked cookies last year landed inside the stomachs of the people in my foreign hometown.

I've decided to put the cookie making biz on hold for a while I finish creating some more cookbooks. So for now I've decided to cook just for myself, family and friends while I finish writing a few more cookbooks.

I'm well aware that there are lots of cookbook junkies out there and maybe there's even a few that bought this book that will probably never read it because they just like to collect all sorts of cookbooks.

What I'd say to them if they could hear me is that they should really cook more and not just buy books because there are so many great recipes in the world hiding in these cookbooks.

My hope is that my cookbook will be an exception, and will become your favorite go to Italian Cookbook when making Italian food. I'm excited about the cookbooks I'm currently working on.

If you're part of my free email club I'll send you an email alert when they become available. The new books will feature many more "famous" fantastic recipes that I believe most people will love.

Finally, since you probably don't know me yet, I should tell you that I'm a pizza freak. I also love Asian food, which means that I need my regular fix of ginger and garlic in addition to tomato sauce.

The first thing I remember as a child was pizza, which I wrote lots about in the beginning chapters of this book.

I guess that's why when I was a baby before I could really speak I used to get tears in my eyes when trying to say the word tomato. My mother didn't understand me for a while but she figured out what I was pointing to and crying for.

Imagine craving something so much before you could talk and had to depend on what someone else could figure out that you wanted?

At least this is the true story that my mother told me. I still love tomatoes but can get them now without tears on my own. Although these days I love them with some salt after removing the skin and seeds, I like to eat them as part of a recipe that uses tomato sauce, like Lasagna, Eggplant Parm, Pasta, Pizza or cooked tomato sauce that I can dip fresh bread into.

I love so many types of pizza. A few of my favs are: Neapolitan, Sicilian, New York Style, Chicago Deep Dish (regular or stuffed), and Barbeque Chicken Pizza.

But a pizza with fresh Mushrooms is one of my absolute favorites. The flavor from the pizza juice mixed together with the mushrooms is very high up on my list because of the unique flavor it creates.

On occasion I'll make a pizza with pineapple and sliced deli turkey meat just to change things up a bit and get that sweet and salty taste going. But my first choice is always a slice of plain cheese New York Style Thin Crust Pizza. And second is a Sicilian Pizza Pie.

On my blog page I show you (with pictures) how to assemble a deli turkey meat pizza which is a good substitution for Canadian bacon. The deli turkey meat tastes pretty good actually on pizza when baked because it has a salty flavor.

Maybe it doesn't sound so good to you, but I like it, and so have many others that tried it, so don't knock it until you've tried it.

I also like a good BBQ Chicken Pizza sometimes. I hope you enjoy all of your pizza eating and maybe one day we can share a slice together.

At the moment I'm focused on getting my next few cookbooks written and published, so I can continue sharing other famous recipes with you.

I think it's important that people get the famous classic recipes under their belt, which are proven and have gained a reputation, then later attempt other recipes or customize their favorites.

Stay in touch if you like through social media or email. The more friends the better.

Whatever you do, make sure to have lots of fun in the kitchen! Stay healthy and happy and blessed.

Ciao ~ Mario

PLEASE WRITE a REVIEW

Did you enjoy this book?

If so would you please take a minute and share your opinion about this book with others?

It helps people that are considering buying a cookbook connect to or find this book by reading reviews posted by others.

A review consisting just a couple of sentences will greatly help, so it doesn't need to be lengthy.

Reviews are so important to us authors and without them people wouldn't trust or buy things.

To write a review just go to my book's detail page from where you originally purchased it.

All reviews for this cookbook are genuine and authentic, so please add yours too.

If you purchased this book from Amazon then just look for the little box close to the bottom of the page that reads "write a review" then click on it. If from somewhere else then please look to see where you can leave a review for others to read.

Thanks in advance for your help

ALSO DON'T FORGET TO JOIN MY FREE CLUB AT

MarioMazzo.com/mazzos-recipe-club

Made in the USA
Monee, IL
22 August 2022